Scout Camp

Also by James Renner

Nonfiction

Little, Crazy Children: A True Crime Tragedy

True Crime Addict: How I Lost Myself in the Mysterious Disappearance of Maura Murray

The Serial Killer's Apprentice

Amy: My Search for Her Killer

Fiction

The Man from Primrose Lane

The Great Forgetting

Muse

SCOUT CAMP

SEX, DEATH, AND SECRET SOCIETIES INSIDE THE BOY SCOUTS OF AMERICA

JAMES RENNER

CITADEL PRESS
Kensington Publishing Corp.
www.kensingtonbooks.com

For W.D. and E.B.

Confronted by their true selves, most men run away screaming.
—Engywook the Gnome, *The Neverending Story*

"I think it's probably time I write about what happened to us at camp," I said. "Before we get any older and I forget something important."

author's note

Most of this story takes place in the summer of 1995. I have recalled specific conversations to the best of my ability. This is how I remember it.

The names of the counselors who worked at Seven Ranges Boy Scout Reservation have been changed to protect their privacy. The names of the dead are real.

I took most of the photographs that appear in this book when I was a teenage Scout attempting to earn the rank of Eagle. The remainder were taken by a fellow Scout in 2004.

now

W ell, I finally hit rock bottom on April 12, 2022. My chart reads: *Severe episode of recurrent major depressive disorder without psychotic features.* My blood pressure was 185 over 120 by the time my Uber dropped me off at Emergency, so I suppose it wasn't all in my head. I remember the nurse with the kind voice who said she would pink-slip me if I didn't sign myself in for the night, so I signed. I was placed in the violent offender wing because they didn't have an empty bed on the quiet side. At least, that's what they told me.

I sobered up during my stay. First time I'd been sober longer than twelve hours in two years. I'm not in AA. I spent enough time in meetings with my mother when I was a kid to know the steps by heart. I keep a copy of the Big Book in my office. Fun fact: The very first AA meeting took place right here in Akron, a mile from where I live. Akron is known for LeBron James, Devo, and Alcoholics Anonymous.

I announced my sobriety in a tweet the day I was released. About an hour later, a man named Norman reached out over DM. I hadn't spoken to him in ten years. *Godspeed,* he wrote. *Life is much better when you are sober for it.*

In 1995, Norman and I were camp counselors at Seven Ranges Boy Scout Reservation, in rural Ohio. When we were kids, he had blond, curly hair he wore tied up with a rubber band. When things got real bad that summer, his jokes were tethers to sanity. We had other things in common. We were both groomed by the same pedophile, for example.

Once again Norman found me when I was rudderless. When I needed help. We made plans to meet halfway between Akron and

Columbus, at a ridiculous Mexican-themed restaurant in Ashland. I've gained nearly a hundred pounds since that summer we were seventeen. He stayed thin. Or maybe he returned to his old self after a while. His hair is cropped short now, all business. He told me how he stopped drinking after working as a videographer for a popular stand-up comic as they toured the United States. "I remember this one night," he said, "an hour outside the Canadian border, and he tells me we have to drink all the alcohol on the bus or Customs will make us throw it out. I'm not even sure if that's true, but we did it." He felt like he'd had enough to drink forever. And after a while he didn't crave it anymore.

After we finished our enchiladas, I got around to the real reason I'd asked to see him.

"I think it's probably time I write about what happened to us at camp," I said. "Before we get any older and I forget something important."

I expected him to talk me out of it. Instead, he nodded and said, "Good."

And so I asked him the question that had been on my mind ever since he had replied to my tweet: "Do you think there's any chance Mike was murdered?"

then

I got my first blow job when I was eleven years old.

This happened at Seven Ranges, in 1989, the summer after fifth grade. One Sunday afternoon my dad dropped me off with a duffel bag full of damp clothes and I marched with the rest of my Boy Scout troop to a nest of canvas tents arranged in two rows at the bottom of a hill. Every troop got its own campsite named after a Native American tribe we stole the land from. Ours was named Wyandotte.

Seven Ranges is a nine-hundred-acre reservation made up of twenty or so campsites like Wyandotte, spread out over an isolated section of Carroll County, a quiet community of Mennonite farmers in Northeast Ohio. It is the largest Boy Scout summer camp in the state, with all manner of activities for boys, including canoeing, swimming, crafts, archery, and guns. It has a large log cabin dining house that seats six hundred Scouts; an ecology center with a collection of amphibians, spiders, and snakes; and a trading post where campers can buy slushies and Combos (cheddar cheese cracker flavor).

After the other boys and I stowed our gear, we changed into swim trunks. Then we grabbed our towels and jogged down to the lake for a swimming test to see if we could tread water. If you passed the test, you got to swim in the deep end beyond the docks for the rest of the week. I grew up on a farm in the country before the Internet, so I already knew how to swim like a fish. I got a special, green-rimmed token with my name on it that I was supposed to hang on a wood board whenever I came to the lake so that lifeguards could keep count of everybody and make sure nobody drowned under the muddy water. It was called a Buddy Tag, because you always had to swim in pairs.

Seven Ranges is a nine-hundred-acre reservation

made up of twenty or so campsites,

spread out over an isolated section of

Carroll County, a quiet community

of Mennonite farmers in Northeast Ohio.

Later that evening my troop attended a Campfire program atop Thunderbird Hill, the highest point in the county, so high you could see all the way to Pennsylvania if you looked real hard. There were magic tricks, I remember, performed by two staffers, who later became important to me: Lucas Taylor and Ben Wilson. Lucas was the magician, Ben the comic relief. Lucas did the red scarf trick, the one where he kept pulling red scarves out of Ben's mouth until you couldn't believe it anymore. After they were done, the campfire died out and all that was left was the amber glow of the embers. Suddenly a drum beat loudly from the surrounding woods. It was impossible to determine its source. The silhouette of a man in a loincloth appeared in front of the dying fire. He spoke in a deep, resonate voice. "In five days you are invited to take part in Pipestone," he said.

I didn't know what Pipestone was, but it sounded wonderfully mysterious.

Afterward, we walked back to our campsite in silence, a tradition that honored the chief of Pipestone. Once we returned to Wyandotte, the youngest Scouts huddled together inside one tent on the fringe of camp. The tents were standard-issue, drab-green, army-surplus tents set atop wooden pallets, each with two steel beds with foam mattresses and wire box springs. Someone pushed the two beds together and we drew straws to see who would sleep on top and who would sleep underneath. I believe there were eight of us. Four up, four down. I got to be up top.

We talked into the early hours of the next day, about Batman and Indiana Jones, about who got stuck with the kiddie swimmer group. We cussed and sang Weird Al Yankovic songs. And then sometime after the first Scout fell asleep, a boy named Craig found my hand under the covers and placed it on his prick.

I felt the thrill of it instantly. A quickening in my chest. There was this thought: *We can do this? This is a thing people do?* The invitation felt very mature, solidly grown-up. When I didn't pull my hand away, Craig responded by reaching over and slipping his hand down my shorts. He cupped my testicles and slowly rotated his fingers. It felt fantastic. After a few minutes of this, he moved down and put his mouth over me.

You should be asking how Craig knew to do this, as he was only eleven himself. I have a strong suspicion that he was abused by someone much older. All I know for sure is that this was clearly not the boy's first time.

In the morning I ventured to the shower house. I had awoken to find myself enveloped in an all-consuming shame. There was a great, heavy weight on my soul. I was a Christian. A Catholic on holidays. But there was something more frightening than an angry God. I knew that if my father ever found out about what had happened in that tent, he'd be furious. We'd taken a family trip to Knott's Berry Farm Theme Park in a rented Winnebago when I was eight, and when we got to the parking lot, I had hung off the back and shouted, "I'm a homo!" because I'd gotten the word mixed up with "hobo" and I was pretending to be the type that hitched rides on a wayward boxcar, and I'd never seen such rage, boy. "Don't ever say that," he yelled. Eventually I figured out my mistake. So I took a shower, trying to wash off the shame. It was one of those open-roofed showers, cement-floored, where you have to push the button for water a couple times before it gets warm. It helped a little, but then Craig came in and got naked, too, and though I was certain I was damned to hell because of it, I watched him jerk off into the drain.

The next several days were filled with merit badge classes and activities. There was time to visit Scoutcraft, where you could walk across a rope bridge and learn how to measure the height of a tree using a piece of paper folded into a triangle, and Handicraft, where you could tie-dye T-shirts and whittle necklaces. I particularly enjoyed Astronomy (on Wednesday night we got to take out the big telescope and take turns looking at craters on the moon while our counselor played the theme from *Star Wars* on the P.A. speaker). For each meal, upon arriving at the dining hall, we were made to tie knots to gain entry. The challenge started out easy enough (square knot), but quickly advanced to clove hitches and sheet bends by the end of the week. My friends and I got around this by passing already-tied knots through a window once one of us got through.

The program director for Seven Ranges that year was a man named Dave Wagner. He was a very serious grown-up who didn't smile much and commanded respect the way a drill sergeant does. Once inside the dining hall, Scouts were instructed to stand quietly behind their chairs, arms crossed, until Wagner began the meal song. Of course, if you put several hundred boys into a confined space, you just know they're going to whisper jokes to each other. When that happened, Dave wouldn't say anything. He'd simply stand silently on the riser at the front of the dining hall, before the great big windows that looked out over the lake. He'd wait. He'd wait and wait and wait, sometimes for ten minutes. Eventually, impatient and hungry, the boys would take note and go quiet. Then Dave would sing the first word of a song and everyone would sing along. In my eyes Dave Wagner was a celebrity on par with Johnny Carson, the emcee and host of the camp. He remained in that role for many years, until he got sick and died of AIDS. So it goes.

Thirty-three years after that summer, it is hard for me to recall much more of that first week other than flashes of images and a feeling of freedom. I recall a giant water balloon war between our troop and the troop next door to Wyandotte—they had catapults that could launch a balloon over the treetops all the way to our tents! However, I do remember Pipestone in exquisite detail.

Friday night, the last night of camp, I joined up with a group of Tenderfoots, who had gathered outside the Admin building. There were maybe fifty of us, most under the age of thirteen. We were told to fold our arms over our chests and walk quietly across the road to the path that led into the woods beyond. Until then, that was a part of camp we'd been forbidden to enter. The sun was setting and the woods were dark, so we walked carefully along the dirt trail over exposed roots and washouts, an adult chaperone up front pointing the way with a flashlight.

Eventually we came to a field of bluegrass. They told us to sit quietly there and then one of the adults built a fire with long, clean sticks they called "faggots." Once the fire was lit, every adult disappeared and we were simply children, abandoned in the woods. What were we supposed to do? How long were we supposed to wait? Nobody had left instructions, other than to remain still, to remain quiet. Eventually the sun vanished and the stars came out and the peepers sang and the fireflies danced and the fire slowly consumed itself until nothing remained besides those glowing embers.

And then the Indians came for us.

now

This is a little awkward, isn't it?

You know me personally now. And I know nothing of you. Chances are, we'll never meet and I'll fade from your mind after you set down this book (or when you toss it across the room round about page 104). But I'm thinking about you. As we move along, I will be constantly concerned about what you're thinking of me and what you think of this story and what you think the point is or whether you identify any themes I might have missed.

Are you wondering, *What have I gotten myself into? What is this book really about?*

It's a true crime book, I think. That's where the bookstores will stock it. There's a suspicious death at its center and lots of other crimes and mysteries sprinkled throughout. I write true crime, but my other books are about some tragedy that happened to someone else: the murder of Amy Mihaljevic, the disappearance of Maura Murray. This story is about crimes that happened to my friends and me.

But this book is also about the Boy Scouts in general and maybe you're curious about that. The Boy Scouts of America (BSA) is an organization so steeped in tradition we rarely give it a second thought. It's become part of the patriotic background. It's a component of the American way of life, like baseball; it's the subject of paintings by Norman Rockwell. It's what boys do here. I think it's strange that we don't think more about the Boy Scouts, because it's a very influential organization. Perhaps the most influential of them all. What other organization openly admits to shaping the psychological development of our children? Maybe the Catholic Church? But let's have some perspective. In the United States, there are about seventeen thousand Catholic parishes. Meanwhile, there are around 150,000 Boy Scout troops and Cub Scout packs. Eagle Scouts, the most indoctrinated of Scouts, often go on to serve in leadership roles in business and government (JFK was the first Scout to become president and there have been six more since). The ideas and ideals that shaped these men's world views began with lessons they learned earning merit badges as boys. We're all looking around for the Illuminati. Brother, here it is. So, yes, I think it's important to take a hard look at why the Boy Scouts was created in the first place, who wrote their books, and what their agenda really is. And we'll get to that.

Because of what I survived, I am keenly aware of how the Boy Scouts' policies led to the events that happened to my friends and me at Seven Ranges. It was the fuel that fed so many fires, real and figurative, leaving one young man dead and oh so many injured, physically and psychologically.

This book is also about recovery—recovery from alcohol and drugs, sure, but also recovery from sexual abuse and coercion, recovery from trauma, and not just mine. And I'm not sure how good of a spokesman I can be. I'm not supposed to drink, but I still do. My doctor says I have drug-seeking behavior and I suppose that's true because I abused opioids this week. I'm not sure I can change or that I want to. You should know that going in. You *don't* have to read this book. I'm telling you that up front because I don't want to find any rage reviews on Goodreads about how you didn't know what you were getting into.

There's one more bit of background I should share that (I think) goes a long way toward explaining some of the choices I made and why. In 1995, at the age of seventeen, I decided to spend a summer away from my family in the woods with a bunch of boys. My mom got pregnant with me when she was a teenager and my parents divorced when I was three. My dad got custody (nasty divorce) and remarried a woman named Linda and we went to live in the country on a one-lane blacktop road that bubbled in the hot summers.

Here's how I learned about the divorce: One day when I was getting ready for bed, my dad handed me the phone. On the other line was my mom. "Your father is going to have you this week," she said. "And then this weekend you'll see me. And then he'll have you every other weekend."

I understand that she was trying to relay this difficult information the best she could. And, grammatically, what she said makes sense if you're an intelligent adult. But being four years old, what I heard was that I'd see my mother that weekend and then never again. My dad would have me "every other weekend" meaning all the other weekends from here to eternity. Keep that in mind, should you ever find yourself on the other end of that phone call.

My mother moved to the city and married a man named Tom and lived in the upstairs of a house where the landlord lived below. By the luck of the draw, I got two abusive stepparents. Linda began hitting me with a closed fist when I was five. Tom never hit me, but on the weekends I spent with my mother, he would sometimes drink Wild Turkey all night and then lay into her while I listened from behind a locked door, too small to do anything to stop it.

I am a child of children. I am the product of my past, like my parents, reaching back to the poor decisions of their parents and theirs, decades and generations back. The past haunts. That's pretty much the only thing I've learned as an adult. The past haunts us. The child I was is the ghost that visits me at night. I sense his unrest in the dark hours.

And I comfort him by telling.

then

I thought the Indians were real. Remember, I was eleven. My capacity to reason was not fully primed and I remember thinking the elders at camp must have done some deal with a local reservation, like maybe they bussed the Indians in every Friday night so they could perform their old rituals to terrorize us kids. Perhaps they even let them take a couple boys to keep the peace. Anyway, they came screaming out of the woods, the orange light of the dying fire reflecting off their dark skin. Red men in loincloths and leather moccasins. They hollered like a war party, the scalping kind. And, yes, I know they are called Native Americans and the tribes in this region of Ohio probably didn't ever scalp anybody, but this was 1989. And the men playing the part were anything but woke. At Seven Ranges, they were always Indians. "Feathers, not dots," as they told us.

The Indians grabbed the little children and pulled them to their feet, twisting their arms into pretzels so that each boy was standing with his arms folded over his chest. I jumped up and stood still and folded my arms before they got to me. An Indian passed by. I could smell his body, rank with sweat in the humid air.

Suddenly there was a loud hissing and I looked to see another Indian holding a lit road flare. Its smoke was strong with sulfur, like those things you get at the fireworks store, the small hockey pucks that transform into snakes when you light them. The Indian with the flare jogged into the woods, creating a cavern of light under a verdant, primordial canopy, down a trail that led farther away from camp. We were instructed (by shoves, by barks, by pointed fingers, but never by words) to follow.

They came screaming out of the woods, the
orange light of the dying fire reflecting off
their dark skin. Red men in loincloths and
leather moccasins.

I joined the others running down the path, which was narrow and turned sharply around large rocks and over knobby roots of century-old trees. They prodded us to move faster, dangerously fast. And now all the Indians had flares and it was impossible to hear anything besides the sizzle of the bright red lights and everything was cast in that cancerous glow and we were the deep shadows racing through the forest.

Around another bend, the boy in front of me slipped and face-planted into the dirt. I dodged to the side—there was no time to stop—but the boy behind me tripped over him and went down, too. Suddenly I was seized. A large Indian grabbed my shoulders from behind and pushed me forward, faster, around the others. Perhaps he misinterpreted what had just happened. Maybe he thought I had caused the other boys to fall, because this seemed like some kind of punishment. He pushed me all the way to the front of the line and then we arrived at a clearing in the forest. A fire raged at the bottom of a slope and what I saw there struck me with bright fear.

A great Indian chief sat on a stump behind a raised fire inside a wire grating the size and shape of a pig's trough. As the sticks burned, their embers fell through the holes and down to the ground like little meteors. The chief wore a headdress of peacock feathers and his fat, red gut drooped over his loincloth. He appeared disinterested in his visitors. He might have been sleeping. Indian dignitaries stood to either side of him, guarding him.

The flares were snuffed out on the ground and I was led down the hill, close enough to the fire that I could feel its heat. The other boys lined up in rows behind me. Whatever was about to happen, it was going to happen to me first.

One of those other Indians, the ones that made up the chief's council, stepped forward, eyes on me. He wore bells around his ankles that announced his every move. He lifted his right hand, palm facing me. I didn't move. All I knew for sure was that anyone who moved got "corrected" by one of their guards.

A moment went by and then another Indian grabbed me and

undid my arms and twisted my hand open so that I was copying the chief's lieutenant. I got it. *Monkey see, monkey do.*

A second Indian lifted a hand. I repeated the action. He motioned for me to step forward. I did so, on wobbly legs. I was unaware of the hundred eyes marking my every move. I was in a ritual and the only thing that existed was the ritual, now, until it was completed. Like Communion. Or the ancient ritual of Chüd. I felt that if I did something wrong, these Indians could make a kid disappear pretty quick. I wondered . . . did my dad know anything about this? Did any of our parents know what they were doing to us?

An Indian handed me a clamshell full of liquid.

"Drink," he whispered. "Spit it out and you fail."

I brought the shell to my lips and sipped, swallowed. Whatever was in it instantly dried up my mouth and puckered my lips. Bitter. More bitter than anything I'd ever tasted before. My mind thought of Clorox bleach, but they wouldn't really make a kid drink bleach, right? I gritted my teeth and swallowed. Many years later, I would learn that what they had us drink that night was Denatonium, commonly known as Bitrex. It's the stuff they put in antifreeze and shampoo so toddlers don't drink it.

I was taken then to a medicine man, who held a stone tablet upon which was written simple commandments. I had to recite them out loud.

"'Before these braves, I promise to tell no other person of this ceremony,'" I said. "'An Indian keeps his word whether good or evil. I go now to the Great Chief to learn the password of this First Degree.'"

I walked to the chief, who was bigger and older than the other Indians. He was morbidly obese. And for the first time, I felt some relief. This was no Indian. I could see that now. This was just a fat white man who'd painted his body. He looked like my bus driver.

I was forced to the ground in front of him. I knelt before the chief, so close that his bare legs flanked me on either side. He turned and brought out a human skull and placed it in front of my face.

"Look inside and see the password to the Second Degree," he said in a low voice. "Do not share this password with anybody or your Pipestone will be taken from you."

I leaned forward, and as I did, a light came on inside the skull, where a man's brains were once stored. On the back of the skull was a single word: *SECRECY.*

"Do you understand?"

"Yes," I replied.

"Return to your people," the chief said. He waved me on to a final Indian, who placed something in my hand. It was small and square and hard, like a rock. I didn't look, though. If I tried to look, one of the other Indians would surely correct me. So I walked quietly to the back of the line with my arms folded.

I watched as the other boys passed through the trials. Occasionally a Scout would spit the bitter juice onto the ground and then several Indians would jump him and pull him back to the line and he'd have to start over. I was aware, too, that our group was smaller than it was when we started. Some of the boys had not made it all the way to the clearing at the end of the path. I felt pride in that.

At some point I realized that my arms were folded so tightly that I was squeezing my chest. It was becoming hard to breathe. Very quietly, aware of every Indian around the fire, I relaxed my grip and breathed in deeply. Oxygen rushed to my brain and I promptly fainted.

When I awoke, I found myself on the ground near the edge of the woods, looking up at another Indian. This one didn't look scary. This one looked genuinely concerned. He could not have been more than sixteen years old.

"Are you okay?" he asked quietly.

"Yes," I said. My head was swimmy, though.

"Can you breathe?"

"Yes."

"Good," he said. He helped me sit up. We were back aways from the ceremony, at the top of the slope. And we were not alone. A couple other Scouts sat quietly nearby, looking on. I could tell that one had been crying. We were the weak ones.

When the last Scout had completed the gauntlet, the chief invited us to come and sit with him at the fire as true braves. We gathered around and he gave a speech about the importance of keeping secrets. Real men kept secrets and we were becoming real men. This was a first step on that journey. But most of all, we must never, ever talk about what happened on this side of the road, of the things that happened at Pipestone.

Then he told us a story about some kind of Indian god, called the "Walk-and-Talk Man," and a goddess known as the Buffalo Calf Woman, who returned to Earth as a white buffalo in times of transformation.

After he was done, the chief commanded us to return to camp and his Indians chased us all the way back to the road and left us there to walk back to our campsites alone, at around three in the morning.

I didn't open my hand until I was safely back inside my tent. I had been so afraid to drop what they'd given me, to lose it on the trail. I'd gripped it so tightly that it left a square mark on my palm. I shone my flashlight on the token.

It was a square of rock, the color of good mud, and upon it was carved a stick-figure man holding a staff above his head, the sigil of the first degree of Pipestone. I had survived. I was a part of some secret and mysterious society now. My first thought was I couldn't wait to tell my father. But then I remembered the chief's warning. If I wanted to become a good man, I must understand the need for secrecy. I could never tell my father.

I wouldn't tell him about Craig, either. Why should I? Real men keep secrets.

now

Thirty-five years later, the Boy Scouts are bankrupt. To understand how it all fell apart, it's important to first understand how it was created. It may surprise you to learn that this pillar of American life was founded by a British war criminal and closeted homosexual who wanted to build a new generation of conservatives to rule the world.

Allow me to explain.

Our story begins with a fortuitous discovery in South Africa, in February 1886. Two men, both named George, had come to build a farmhouse near a river full of whitewater in a region of good land in the southern part of the continent that was owned by the Dutch. Their people were the Boers, which is Dutch for "farmer." One Sunday, according to subjective and very old affidavits, George Walker went for a stroll around the farm. On his walk he tripped over an outcropping of rock and tumbled to the ground. He looked back to find a piece of the large rock had broken off. It glittered in the sun. That glimmer pulled at his curiosity like the One Ring had called to Sméagol. And like the ring, it was better left unfound.

Walker had discovered gold. And not a little. In fact, that outcropping of rock was only the tip of one branch of a great golden reef that stretched in an arc along the shores of a prehistoric lake. He had discovered, *literally stumbled upon,* the largest gold reserves on the entire planet. Word traveled. Soon that little farm was the epicenter of a great gold rush. And while the gold remained under Dutch control, the British Empire grew covetous.

The Crown owned much of the rest of South Africa at the time,

including the Cape Colony at the tip. The Dutch had left the cape after
Great Britain abolished slavery, trekking inland to search for fertile
country where they could be left alone to toil the land using human
stock—Black men taken from indigenous tribes. As Cape Town grew,
the British Empire expanded around the Dutch independent states so
that they were nearly surrounded.

The discovery of limitless gold seemed like a blessing to the Boers
at first. After all, money was power on the frontier. But these farmers had no experience refining minerals. Neither did their slaves. So
they hired foreigners. And as it happened, the most skilled refiners
were British. It quickly became apparent to Dutch leaders that the
Brits would soon outnumber their own people inside their African
territories. To secure political control, the Dutch levied taxes on the
immigrants and would not grant them the right to vote.

Wars of legend were started over less.

Meanwhile, the Empire began to amass troops along the borders.
They stockpiled munitions. But the Boers had an advantage—their
citizens were trained gunmen and, at least for the moment, they out-
numbered their enemy. As such, it was advantageous to the Dutch to
attack first, before the British could send reinforcements from home.

On October 12, 1899, the Boers invaded Cape Colony. British
troops retreated. The Boers pushed inward, targeting stores of supplies they could reappropriate for their own army. Around eight thousand Dutch farmers armed with rifles made for the town of Mafeking,
which was a central transportation hub the Brits used to send arms
and food to towns all across South Africa.

But Mafeking had an eccentric leader, who had prepared a small
group of soldiers and townsfolk for just such an attack. The man's personal motto had always been "Be prepared." Thus, the Siege of Mafeking began and the Boers and the world were introduced to Colonel
Robert Baden-Powell.

Baden-Powell was a city kid from Paddington, London. His father
was a Church of England priest and professor of geometry at Oxford,
who died when his son was just three years old, leaving him in the sole

care of his mother, Henrietta Grace, a woman obsessed with maintaining an upper-class lifestyle in spite of her husband's passing.

His mother called him Stephe, pronounced "Stevie." Stephe was a different sort of boy. He liked to play with dolls. In early photographs he's seen wearing dresses and could easily be mistaken for a girl. He had many siblings, some of whom died young. His family was insular, and stronger for this. Henrietta Grace taught her children the importance of supporting family above all things. From a young age they shared a communal cashbox from which incidental money could be taken and any money earned deposited. When her boys became adults, Henrietta kept her fingers tangled up in their affairs, especially Stephe, whose life she shaped in many ways.

"The whole secret of my getting on lay with my mother," Stephe later said. There is little doubt that Henrietta Grace was the most important woman in his life, the one with whom he had the closest emotional bond. Stephe was driven by the need for her approval. "There is only one pain greater than that of losing your mother," he once said. "And that is the pain your mother would suffer if she lost you. I do not mean by death but by your own misdeeds."

Young Stephe studied piano and violin, and when he was old enough, he was sent to a fancy, all-boy's school called Charterhouse, in Surrey, where he lived most of the year. If you're picturing Hogwarts, you're not far off. The school is practically a castle, situated in the quiet countryside. Discipline at Charterhouse was meted out by prefects instead of the adult staff, and the older boys had authority to spank the younger students. And though homosexuality was taboo at school, it was common for younger students to seek out older boys for protection, even if it meant using attraction as a means of commerce. In this style Stephe befriended an older boy named Parry, who later said that he was quite fond of Stephe's "pair of twinkling eyes."

It was at Charterhouse that Stephe discovered a love for the theater, and he often played the roles of women, such as the landlady in a play called, ahem, *Cox and Box* when he was fifteen.

It's fascinating to peer back into Stephe's life in his many biographies and see how he developed and how he crossed paths with so many influential figures of the time, people like Winston Churchill and Mahatma Gandhi, though these chance encounters appeared mundane before history and hindsight imbued them with special meaning. For instance, when Henrietta Grace discovered that Stephe was falling behind in his maths, she sent her son to a tutor named Charles Lutwidge Dodgson, a man who had authored a couple mathematical proofs. You probably know Mr. Dodgson by his pen name—Lewis Carroll. But did you know that the main character in his book *Alice's Adventures in Wonderland* was based off a real girl, named Alice Liddell, whom Carroll often photographed in the nude before she reached puberty?

After school Stephe enlisted in the army and was sent to India, where he gained notoriety for the theater productions he produced to entertain the troops; he even put on a revival of *Cox and Box*. The army once granted Stephe leave from war to act a part in a play written by the father of the viceroy of India.

While stationed in Quetta, which is now a part of Pakistan, Stephe produced several new plays starring a young officer named Kenneth McLaren, who acted in drag for the female roles. McLaren was twenty but looked about fourteen. Stephe nicknamed him "the Boy." A slew of circumstantial evidence suggests that the Boy was the love of Stephe's life.

Tim Jeal, the preeminent biographer of Lord Baden-Powell, devotes an entire chapter to the charged relationship between the leader of the Boy Scouts and young McLaren. Jeal was granted access to troves of Baden-Powell's personal correspondence by his descendants during his research that revealed a very close relationship between the pair.

Jeal wrote that while the two were starring together in a production of *The Pirates of Penzance*, Stephe would often return to his hut to find the Boy asleep in Stephe's own bed. And when their regiment was transferred to Mutta, the Boy shared a bungalow with Stephe. They made a home together and took in a couple dogs and a pet pig named Algernon. McLaren liked to gift Stephe silk handkerchiefs.

And so, some years later, when Stephe was called back to Africa to protect the British Empire from the Boers, the Boy came with him.

It should be noted that by the time of the Siege of Mafeking, Stephe's reputation within the military was in tatters. He'd narrowly escaped prosecution the last time he was on the African continent for killing the god of the Makalaka people. The Makalakas' divine leader, Chief Uwini, had led a resistance against British colonialism, and while defending his people, he was captured by Stephe's troops. Instead of sending Uwini to a court for a proper trial, Stephe formed an ad-hoc war tribunal, sentenced the chief to death, and killed him by firing squad, to send a message to the Makalaka rebels. Many viewed this as both deicide and a war crime. Stephe was later cleared of wrongdoing by the military.

It was around this time that Stephe began recording his personal wisdom into books. In 1884, he published *Reconnaissance and Scouting*, a field guide for army scouts about how to gather intelligence on their enemies.

Near the turn of the century, when the Empire's relationship with the Boers dissolved, Stephe was commanded to lead a mobile unit of soldiers to engage with Dutch farmers along the northern borders in an effort to draw forces away from the vulnerable south. The Brits needed time to muster an army to properly defend the Cape Colony. But when Stephe saw the stores of goods at Mafeking, he went against orders and decided to defend the town instead of remaining mobile. This decision has divided his biographers. Some believe it was a prescient move, since it accomplished his mission of keeping Boer forces occupied in the north. But others see it as Stephe looking out for number one. He had a better chance of survival by hiding himself in a well-fortified town than he did picking fights on the open plains. In any event the siege began on October 13, 1899, and lasted 217 days.

The numbers were decidedly in favor of the Boers, who arrived at Mafeking with upward of eight thousand armed farmers against a ramshackle one-thousand-men defense. But the Boers were unaware of just how few men Mafeking really had because Stephe waged clever psychological warfare to inflate his numbers and provisions. As the Boers arrived, they spotted Stephe's men burying hundreds of "mines" around the perimeter of the town. In fact, the mines were only boxes filled with sand. At night the enemy would see searchlights moving around the streets; impressive at a distance, but in reality nothing more than oil lamps and cookie tins. His soldiers even built a dummy fort with fake guns to draw fire away from their real battery.

As the siege wore on, Stephe enlisted the help of the teenage boys from Mafeking to supplement the work done by the adult troops. He sent the boys on errand missions and to help at the hospital. He gave them khaki uniforms to wear to distinguish them from civilians. These first "boy scouts" faced real dangers in a very real war; in place of merit badges, their reward was living another day. To pass the time, Stephe wrote and published a new book, *Aids to Scouting*, a guide for military recruits on the subject of survival skills and self-reliance.

There's more to this long siege, another book's worth of escapades. But what's important to know is that for its duration, as his forces were depleted and morale waned, Stephe never blinked. Except for once, that is, very near the end, when the Boy was gravely wounded and captured by the enemy. When he heard the news, Stephe ran toward the border zone and had to be restrained. He pleaded with the Boer leader for a truce. He wrote a letter to his mother at this time, stating: *It is so horrible to sit here within sight of his hospital and yet not be able to see him and help to soothe him.*

Stephe sent letters to the Boy via diplomatic channels to let him know he could never forget him: *Your two photos are the only ornaments on my table as I write.*

After studying the man's writings in detail, Jeal confidently concluded that "Baden-Powell was a repressed homosexual." However, he suggested the relationship with McLaren might never have been physical. The shame of such an act may have been too much to initiate, he thought. I'm not so sure. That's a long time in a small house in the middle of nowhere.

Stephe and the Boy were reunited after the siege ended with the British victorious. When Stephe returned home to England, he was welcomed as a war hero. And he discovered that in his absence something odd had happened. His book, *Aids to Scouting,* had become a bestseller. And it seemed to be particularly popular with teenage boys.

Meanwhile, in the United States, society was in tremendous upheaval. The Industrial Revolution had changed everything. Families were moving from the farms into cities. Boys who once worked the fields were now obliged to go to school and had plenty of extra time to get into trouble. Responding to this, some towns formed youth groups to fill the children's idle hours and to further promote religion and patriotism that would bolster what was taught in schools— groups like London, England's YMCA (Young Men's Christian Association) and the American-based Woodcraft Indians, an organization begun in Connecticut, in 1901, that reappropriated Native American traditions into a club for white boys.

Stephe heard about the Woodcraft Indians and imagined a similar organization for boys in England. In 1907, he invited twenty young men to camp with him on Brownsea Island in Dorset Poole Harbour. He gifted each of them a khaki scarf and divided them into patrols. They played capture the flag and practiced survival skills. It was a social experiment and in Stephe's eyes it could not have gone better. And so he edited his old book and released it in 1908 as *Scouting for Boys.* It became the manual for the Boy Scouts for the first few years. The movement spread . . . like what? Like good news? Like wildfire? Like a disease? Take your pick.

The Boy Scouts of America was founded in 1910 and soon smaller, separate groups, like the Woodcraft Indians, got swallowed up by the zeitgeist of Lord Baden-Powell's popular Boy Scouts.

Scouting for Boys taught the conservative values that were being neglected in the Progressive Era: patriotism, nationalism, self-reliance, deference to elders, and respect for God. But Stephe also wanted to make sure that boys didn't masturbate.

Initially Stephe planned to include a whole chapter about masturbation in the first printing of the Boy Scout manual, which is now archived on Google Books. "You all know what it is to have at times a pleasant feeling in your private parts and there comes an inclination to work it up with your hand," he wrote. "It is especially likely to happen when you see a dirty picture or hear dirty stories and jokes." He warned boys that if they did this too much, it would cause them to go insane. Luckily, a boy could always talk to his scoutmaster about these things. "If at first you find a difficulty about it don't be afraid to go and talk openly to your officer about it and he will tell you what to do." However, his publisher said, and I'm paraphrasing here, "Hell no."

What remained in the 1911 handbook, which can be found on the Project Gutenberg's website, is watered down, but still bizarre. "In the body of every boy who has reached his teens, the Creator of the universe has sown a very important fluid," it reads. "This fluid is the most wonderful material in all the physical world. This is the sex fluid." The sex fluid, it says, gives a boy his strength and intelligence. And it should never be mismanaged: "Any habit which a boy has that causes this fluid to be discharged from the body tends to weaken his strength, to make him less able to resists disease and often unfortunately fastens upon him habits which later in life he cannot break."

In case you're curious, things did not end well for Stephe and the Boy. McLaren married a young woman who was nice enough to Stephe, but she died from multiple sclerosis before she turned thirty. After that, McLaren became engaged to his deceased wife's nurse, a lower-class woman who didn't care for Stephe and didn't invite him to their wedding. In response to this shunning, Stephe never spoke to the Boy again. A few years later, McLaren slipped into a deep depression and died inside a mental hospital.

Eventually Stephe married as well. In 1912, at the age of fifty-five, he wed twenty-three-year-old Olave St. Clair Soames. She cut her hair and dressed as a boy for him and they had three children, but Stephe could not stand to sleep with her. It gave him terrible headaches and he took to sleeping on their balcony. In an effort to discover why he reacted so viscerally to sharing a bed with his wife, he consulted a psychologist, who suggested he keep a dream journal. Sometimes, he wrote, he dreamed of being whipped by young men who wished to "discipline" him, according to Jeal.

As he grew older and more famous, the face of the worldwide Boy Scout movement, he often inspected Scout camps around the countryside. He particularly liked to go down to the swimming holes, where the boys swam naked. And he visited old friends like A.H. Tod, a teacher at Charterhouse. Tod kept a collection of photographs of nude boys, which Stephe enjoyed perusing. One letter from Stephe to Tod showed his excitement about returning as soon as he could so that he might possibly "get a further look at those wonderful photographs" of Tod's.

By the time he was eighty years old, Stephe had developed a habit of corresponding with Boy Scouts about masturbation, according to letters found by Tim Jeal, which are no longer public. He also advised curious scoutmasters on the subject. One leader wrote to Stephe, asking if it was permissible to fondle a boy in order to show him that such a thing was natural. There's no indication that Stephe shared this letter with anyone in authority, but he did advise the man that he should work at "that deeper form of subordination of one's own desires."

As his health began to fail, Stephe returned to Africa, staying at a hotel in Kenya that was owned by a friend. "I'd rather die in Africa, where my heart is," he said. He died on January 8, 1941, at the age of eighty-three.

The Official Boy Scout Handbook has become one of the top-selling books in history, with over 40 million copies printed. Baden-Powell's personal philosophies have influenced the minds of generations of boys throughout the world. And maybe, just maybe, the reason there are so many pedophiles in the Boy Scouts is because the Boy Scouts was founded by a man who was, himself, scouting for boys.

then

On August 20, 1994, a white buffalo was born at a farm in Janes-
ville, Wisconsin. It was named Miracle and Native Americans hailed
it as the fulfillment of the promises of old. It was an omen of change.
When I heard the news, I couldn't wait to return to Seven Ranges to
complete my fifth and final year of Pipestone and to be part of the
crew that created the program that was inspired by this legend.

Every summer I had asked my father if I could work at Seven
Ranges. The camp sometimes took on younger Scouts as counselors-in-training, or CITs. I wished to sleep in tents and have adventures. Mostly, I wanted to disappear into the woods because I wished
to live deliberately away from my stepmother's shadow. And each year
my father told me I was too young. But in the summer of 1995, I
signed myself up and told him I had made up my mind to go. I was
seventeen and old enough to make my own choices. He was still hes-
itant, but he didn't stop me.

"I have a bad feeling about that place," he told me. "Be careful. Be
aware of your surroundings."

I promised him I would, even as I immediately dismissed his con-
cern. He was being paranoid. What could possibly go wrong? I didn't
think of what happened to me the first night I ever spent at that camp.
I had become quite adept at pushing the memory of my first sexual
experience down into the deepest recesses of my mind. And all things
being equal, camp was still safer than home.

Linda wasn't hitting me anymore. They stop that when you get
taller than them, don't they? Instead, she screamed at me. And I
would answer in kind. We would yell at each other for hours until we

I couldn't wait to return to Seven Ranges
to complete my fifth and final year of Pipestone
and to be part of the crew that created the program
that was inspired by this legend.

were both weak and exhausted by hate. She screamed at me if I didn't finish my dinner. She screamed at me if I spent too much time in my room reading Robert McCammon. She'd accuse me of doing drugs if I played my *Doors Greatest Hits* cassette tape too loudly.

When I was little, I wondered why she didn't like me. By the age of seventeen, I didn't care. I'd become cruel to her, but only after many years of this. This relationship is the central crux of my ongoing therapy.

"She did the best she could with the tools she had at the time," Dr. Deb has told me. And sometimes I believe that to be true.

"Nobody is happy like you are," Linda said to me once. "You have to be doing drugs."

But no, not then. I *really was* that happy.

I remember this petty drama that happened among the political ranks of the soccer moms at school one fall. Linda was a volunteer with the soccer program, working the concession stands during Saturday games. There were six of them in this group, mothers of soccer players. At the end of every season, one of the moms would print out a master record of that year's games, with wins/losses for each team, in a folded paper program we kept as a souvenir. My younger sister, our parents, and I were eating at the kitchen table, and Linda showed an early version of the program to my dad.

"Look at this," she said, pointing to one team's season record. "The program's messed up. The Sharks didn't win a single game. But the program has them with one win."

"Hmm," my dad said. "Who printed the program?"

"Sharon," she replied.

And before I could stop myself, I said, "She did it on purpose." And look, it doesn't matter. That lady was trying to make a better season for the Sharks, inflating the score just enough to make it not embarrassing, so that it wasn't a complete shutout. What she did was a venial sin at best.

"No, she wouldn't do something like that on purpose," said Linda.

"Sharon's son is a Shark, right?"

"Right. But she told me she just slipped when she was typing it up and accidentally hit the 1 instead of the 0."

"But the 1 is on the opposite side of the keyboard from 0," I said.

"No. Why would 0 be on the other side? The 0 is always next to 1."

I walked to my room, got my typewriter, and returned. When they saw the row of numbers, my father started laughing.

"The kid's eight years old and he's the only one who could figure out she's lying?"

My dad was laughing. But Linda wasn't. That was one of the first times I saw open hatred there.

My father drove me to camp one day in early June, that summer I was seventeen, my duffel bag scooting around the back of his pickup. The road to camp winds through the hills of rural Ohio, through great pastoral paintings: fields of corn and soy, cows chewing cud. It meanders through towns no more than a dot on a folded map, nothing more than a gas station on a corner, places frozen in time since World War II, in-the-middle-of-nowhere ice-cream stands selling soft serve for fifty cents.

The gravel parking lot for camp is off a dirt road where Mennonites live. There's a long ranch-style building with slat board siding there called Administration. One half is the main office. The other half is a First Aid station. By the time I arrived, hundreds of Scouts were already milling about outside, waiting to be processed into camp one troop at a time, everyone in their formal, Class-A uniforms, those khaki button-up shirts with the red epaulets. Some older boys also wore merit badge sashes. Camp counselors inspected bags for contraband and any radios or pocket video games were handed back to the parents. This was week one of an eight-week summer, so there was extra energy in the air, a feeling of great beginnings, of marvelous possibility. Everyone was smiling, staff and Scouts alike. This group of kids would stay from Sunday to next Saturday morning and then a new batch of six hundred Scouts from across Ohio would arrive and the cycle would begin anew.

My dad helped me get my duffel bag out of the back and then he warned me one last time. "Watch out for yourself," he said. "Don't let anything happen, because if something bad happens, I will have to come back here and burn this place down. Okay?"

"Promise," I said.

I went into the Admin building to check myself in. There's a smell that is particular to Admin—old, polished wood and astringent, industrial cleaning products. Whenever I encounter this smell to this day, in truck stop bathrooms or National Park visitor centers, my mind swims and for a moment I think I'm still there, at Seven Ranges and everything since has been a fever dream. I found the camp director in the back office, a man with a sharp wit whom everyone called Scooter.

"Renner! You're a week late," he said. "What gives?" The rest of the camp staff had come a week early for setup.

"Family vacation," I said. "I mentioned it in the interview."

"I figured you went AWOL, so I fired you." He held his glare for a second more, then smiled.

"Oh, well, could you rehire me then?"

Scooter sighed dramatically. "Fine. You'll have to take a tent in CIT-ville until we find you better accommodations."

Gross. CIT-ville was below the dining hall, hidden behind a nest of never-pruned pine trees. No view. No electricity. "All right," I said.

"Oh, and you're teaching First Aid."

"I am?"

He tossed me the instruction manual for the merit badge. "Easy-peasy," he said. "Nine a.m., right behind Admin."

"Okay, then."

"Pick a tent, then head over to the Trading Post, see if they need any help."

"Right."

"Dismissed."

I walked out the back of Admin, passing through a crowd of Scouts loading Pipestone "squaw wood" onto the back of a tractor. In order to take part in the Pipestone ceremonies, Scouts were required

This was week one of an eight-week summer, so there was extra energy in the air, a feeling of great beginnings, of marvelous possibility.

to bring a bundle of sticks with them. A counselor checked each for quality and if there was any bark present on the wood, or if their sticks were too knobby or twisted, the pieces were tossed and that boy was given a few days to find better sticks in the woods around camp.

A wide gravel road led away from Admin down a hill lined with hand-carved wooden signs (like those old Burma Shave ads) that listed all the tenets of the Scout Law: *A Scout is trustworthy, loyal, help-ful, friendly* . . . I walked the road, crunching pebbles underfoot. At the first intersection was a large rock hanging from another sign. This was what passed as a weather station at camp. If the rock was wet, the forecast called for rain; if it was swinging, the forecast was high winds (you get it). I continued to the right, toward the dining hall, which sat atop the next rise, overlooking Lake Donahey. As I rounded a bend, I saw a troop of Scouts walking in step formation down by Waterfront, heading for one of the campsites in the Back Forty, which is what we called the forty acres farthest from Admin. I continued past the dining hall to a nearly invisible path that brought me to CIT-ville.

CIT-ville consisted of six pistachio-green military-style canvas tents atop wooden pallets, three on each side. Under a giant pine canopy was a seventh tent, typically occupied by the senior coun-selor whose job it was to look after the young recruits. CIT-ville was deserted, everyone off to different jobs for check-in. I dropped my duffel inside an empty tent and spread my sleeping bag out on a steel-spring bed.

I headed for the Trading Post then, daydreaming of the potenti-alities of the summer. I felt like I was joining the cast of a beloved TV series. At Seven Ranges the visiting Scouts admired the staffers like they were celebrities. They were actors, teachers, and comedians. The very best counselors were all those in one. It was thrilling that some-one thought it possible that I could be those things as well.

My thoughts drifted to other bright prospects. I was hoping to see a particular boy again, someone I'd met the previous summer. My troop had come out during week four that year, and one evening when everyone had gathered in the dining hall for dinner, the staff had performed a risqué but beloved Irish drinking song called "Little Brown Mouse," which began, "Ohhhhh, the liquor was spilled on the barroom floor and the bar was closed for the night!" It was about how this mouse had a bit too much to drink and went looking to pick a fight with a big tomcat. Anyway, during the song a boy from another troop got up and sang with the staff and upstaged the senior counselors. He was a natural performer. No insecurity, no hesitation. I watched him and felt a kaleidoscope of butterflies in my stomach, that feeling I typically got when I sat next to a girl I liked at school. He had straight red hair and a puckish smile and I saw him a couple more times that week, passing by on the gravel trail or swimming at Watercraft and I got to know him enough to know his name: Trey. Every time I thought of him, a terrible conflict occurred inside my mind. I'd imagine holding his hand in the dark and then I'd immediately become so entangled with icy strands of shame that I'd have to stop before I threw up. If my father knew what I was thinking, if he could see inside the theater of my mind, I was afraid he'd stop loving me. It's that simple. But that's how it was. Please understand, my dad was my only constant in life. Everything else could fall apart (and sometimes did), but in the end it was always the two of us against the world. I owed it to him to keep my mind clean. A Boy Scout is supposed to be "mentally awake and morally straight," after all.

The new Trading Post sat at the top of a hill halfway back to Admin, a long building that was half gift shop, half concession stand. The old Trading Post used to stand over by CIT-ville, but it had been destroyed in a fire two years before. I remember coming that summer and running to the Trading Post to get some snacks, only to find a pile of blackened rubble. They said it was arson, but nobody had been caught.

In the summer of '95, Mark Hower, an interesting fellow who went to Yale, ran the new Trading Post. His parents had died in a tragic accident when they crossed a poorly marked train track on a country road, and I don't think he had anyone outside of camp. I believe he came to Seven Ranges to surround himself with friends, and to that end we all should have been nicer to him. But he had this air about him. Some might use the word "prissy." Probably this guy was just more cultured than the rest of us rubes.

Mark was thankful to have me on his crew and he introduced me to my coworkers, Norman Weber, a tall sixteen-year-old with blond hair tied up with a rubber band, and David Hanlon, a skinny boy with acne and a squeaky voice. They showed me the ropes: how to switch out the syrups for the pop, where to get more boxes of Airheads, and how to change the ribbon on the register. Norman showed me a secret alcove in the rafters, where you could nap if nobody was looking.

"What'll it be?" David asked when the tour was done. He motioned to the slushie machine, with its cylinders of neon-colored frozen sodas.

"How's about a suicide?" said Norman.

In camp parlance a suicide was when you mixed every flavor together. "Sounds great," I said. It was delicious, but that doesn't give it justice, and here's why: When we are seventeen, our senses are still keen. I'm forty-five now and my hearing has gone muffled, my eyesight has gone to shit, and all the things I taste are not so sweet. But at seventeen my body was pristine and sixteen ounces of frozen sugar was divine. It was my favorite drug at camp and I overdosed every day.

And then the last Trading Post employee arrived.

"Sorry I'm late," he said, jumping through the concession stand window and helping himself to a slushie.

My face went red and I swallowed wrong and started coughing.

"Oh yeah," said Norman, "This is Trey. Trey, this is James Renner."

now

I kept everything. Photographs, phone numbers, police reports, my fifth-year Pipestone token. Everything. I put it all into a box after the summer of '95 and it followed me to college, then to my first apartment, and finally into my first house, where I secreted it into the farthest reaches of my basement. I knew, even at seventeen, that there was a story in there and that one day I might understand what that story was. I didn't expect it would take nearly thirty years to find the confidence to look inside again.

The boy I was still lives inside me. Sometimes I feel no different at all and I think I'm still 130 pounds, with a full head of thick hair and limitless energy. Then I catch a glimpse of myself in the bedroom mirror and the years come slamming back all at once. I'm over two hundred pounds, with gray hair and the stuff up top has gone thin.

I don't know where my friends have gone.

I need to find them.

The truth about what happened at Seven Ranges exists as fragments within our separate memories. There are answers out there, even now. I can feel it. I'm also aware that I'm about to ruin some people's peace with the simple message "Hi, it's Renner, can we talk about what happened in 1995?"

I found Trey on Instagram. He's somewhere in Sweden. His posts are landscape photographs of snowcapped mountains and the aurora borealis over a country lake. There's one picture of his face in profile. I think he looks like David Caruso.

I found Tommy on Insta, too. I should probably contact him

before anyone else. It's his story more than any of ours, I guess. He's married with kids. Do they know?

Hey, old friend, I wrote. *I wanted to let you know that I'm chipping away at a book about the summer of '95 . . .*

Tommy read my message that night, but he never replied. I'm not going to push. Maybe he'll reach out one day. Maybe he won't. It's a dangerous time to be a Boy Scout.

The abuse scandal within the Boy Scouts of America has been compared to that of the Catholic Church, but that's not an accurate comparison. The numbers have not been given proper context. The 2004 John Jay Report, which quantified abuse cases within the Church, logged about eleven thousand victims. In the United States, as of this writing, over eighty-two thousand Scouts have filed abuse claims against the Boy Scouts of America. This scandal is exponentially larger in scale, and yet there are no movies about it, no plays yet written. But like the situation within the Catholic Church, the people in power kept this abuse quiet for decades.

The first major news story to shine light on the systemic problem of sexual abuse inside the Boy Scouts of America came out in May 1991, when the *Washington Times* published a five-part investigative series, "Scout's Honor," by the journalist Patrick Boyle. It begins with this straightforward introduction: "For parents, the local Boy Scout troop is a safe place to send the kids. For child molesters, it's an ideal place to meet them."

Boyle's series revealed how the Boy Scouts of America was able to dodge responsibility for the rampant pedophilia in their ranks by franchising its program, turning it into the McDonald's of youth groups. It granted charters to communities around the country, allowing them to form official Boy Scout troops at local churches. But no one at the executive level personally selected scoutmasters—that was all handled locally. So the individual troops ought to be ones on the hook for bringing in child molesters, its lawyers argued, not the executives. And for a while, then, that argument held. The board of directors, in fact, did everything it could to keep that defense in place for as long as possible, hiring a law firm out of Florida to dispatch attorneys to monitor abuse cases across the United States, not to represent the victims, but to advise the small-town lawyers representing local troops on how best to win their case and keep it quiet. Whenever possible, the Boy Scout troops settled out of court and paid the families a settlement in exchange for not discussing the horrific details in public. Their spin when questioned was that such publicity would be bad for the victim. "Our interest is to protect the kid," the director of administration for the Boy Scouts told Boyle.

If their interest really was protecting the kids, they should have spent that money vetting their scoutmasters. Boyle's investigation revealed abuse allegations against Scout leaders in all fifty states and the District of Columbia. He also found that local Scout leaders often decided not to contact police in order to protect the pristine image of the Boy Scouts of America.

When a South Carolina Scout leader was arrested for taking pictures of naked children in 1982, the local Scout executive, Chubby Earnest, wrote this message to Paul Ernst, then director of registration for the Boy Scouts of America: *So far, we have received no bad publicity from this. We'll keep our fingers crossed.*

To which Ernst replied, *I hope the media maintains its silence relating to his involvement with Scouting.*

The *Washington Times* report forever linked pedophilia to the Boy Scout program within the American consciousness. Around this time Adam Sandler began playing a character named Canteen Boy on *Saturday Night Live*. In a sketch from 1994 that has aged like milk, host Alec Baldwin tries to molest Canteen Boy, who escapes by running into the woods. It was played for laughs, but the joke only works (as far as it does) because we all understand that this is what happens on many Boy Scout campouts.

Then along came a man named Kerry Lewis, one victim who refused to settle. In the 1980s, Lewis had been a Scout with Southeast Portland Troop 719, which was sponsored by a local Mormon church. The troop's scoutmaster was a man named Timur Dykes. Dykes was a particularly prolific monster, but not without a conscience. He confided in a Mormon bishop in 1983 that he'd molested at least seventeen boys, one of whom was Kerry Lewis. The bishop accepted his confession. And did nothing. Dykes returned to leading the troop and promptly molested two more Scouts. That finally put Dykes on an "ineligible volunteer" list maintained at the head office of the Boy Scouts of America. But following his release from prison on sodomy charges, in 1988, Dykes was able to return to Scouting and began molesting boys again. Lewis's case was featured in Hulu's recent documentary, *Leave No Trace: A Hidden History of the Boy Scouts.* In April 2010, a jury awarded Lewis $18.5 million, the largest punitive damages awarded in a child abuse case in the United States at that time.

And then something monumentally audacious happened. During the discovery phase of Lewis's case, the Boy Scouts of America provided his lawyers with their ineligible volunteer documents, the so-called "perversion files." Within those 14,500 pages were the names of abusive scoutmasters going back decades, most beyond the statute of limitations for any civil or criminal justice. So Lewis's attorneys, Kelly Clark and Paul Mones, released the files on the Internet for everyone to see. By making the files public, they instigated a reckoning that is still reverberating today. All of those cases that the Boy Scouts of America had fought so hard to keep secret, all of them came out at once, separate fissures in a giant dam that no longer had the structural foundation to repair itself. No matter where you called home, there was an abuser within those files who lived nearby. In the span of a few weeks, news stations all across the United States featured an abuse case from their local troop. Many were so old, the abusers could not be prosecuted due to statutes of limitations. But for the first time, we glimpsed the scale of this horror. That was the beginning of the end.

In response to the outcry over the lack of justice due to statutes of limitations, several states rewrote their laws to allow victims to sue the Boy Scouts for old crimes. Every day a new victim stepped forward and a new lawsuit was filed. It was *lingchi,* death from a thousand cuts. And so, in February 2020, the Boy Scouts of America, once a symbol of purity and reverence, filed for bankruptcy to save itself.

then

At camp there's this ritual that happens each night after dinner. It's called Retreat. Like much of the pomp of Scouting, Retreat is a tradition so old we have forgotten how it started and why we do it. In fact, it's a holdover from Lord Baden-Powell's days in the British Army, where "beating retreat" was the call for soldiers to come inside the fort so that the gates could be closed for the night, protecting the monarch's subjects from the barbarians outside.

Here's how it works. On a plateau below the dining hall, each troop arranges into rows in front of three flagpoles, the Stars and Stripes in the middle. A bugle player performs a shaky rendition of the Retreat melody and the entire staff of Seven Ranges comes marching from around the back of the dining hall, two by two, to the parade grounds, their feet in lockstep, their boots beating the dirt like snare drums.

That was the first year I marched with the staff. I fell in line beside Trey that night. I had no rhythm, however, and keeping in step with him took all of my attention. As we rounded the turn toward the flags, I could feel the eyes of the assembled Scouts upon us. Three senior staffers stood at the flagpoles, awaiting our arrival: Scooter, the camp director, and two other adults I remembered from years past: the magician, Lucas Taylor, and his assistant, Ben Wilson. Ben was the program director in 1995, the emcee of all events. Lucas was now the camp chaplain. Lucas was positioned by a cannon loaded with a blank shotgun shell. In one hand he held a rope that was attached to its trigger, waiting for the moment to pull.

At camp there's this ritual that happens

each night after dinner.

It's called Retreat.

"Company, halt!" said Ben, his voice echoing across the lake and back. "Color guard, retire the colors!"

Four senior staff members stepped forward. One marched to the state flagpole on the right, one went to the camp flag at the left, and the remaining two flanked the American flagpole in the center. The bugle played "Colors," and the camp flag and state flag (actually, in Ohio, it's a pendant) came down.

"Salute!" shouted Ben.

Lucas pulled the rope and the cannon blasted so loud it set my ears ringing. The American flag came down and was quickly folded into a triangle and presented to Ben for inspection. He nodded and the four staffers returned to the line.

"Scoutmasters, take charge of your troops. Camp dismissed!"

The Scouts returned to their campsites then, but just long enough to change into jeans and long-sleeved flannels and sweaters. Sundays always ended with that hour-long Campfire program full of skits and songs to get everyone into the camp spirit. By 1995, the Sunday night Campfire had moved to a new amphitheater that looked out over Lake Donahey. It was timed so that the sunset occurred during the program, and by the time it was over, a first night had come to Seven Ranges.

To warm up the crowd as the straggler troops made their way in, the junior counselors sang "The Bubble Gum Song," a parody of "Choo'n Gum," by Dean Martin. "My mother gave me a penny, to go and see Jack Benny . . ."

And Scouts, hundreds of them, sang along, pantomiming pulling strings of gum between their fingers, stretching it longer and longer after each verse.

There were cheers. The watermelon cheer required everyone to pretend to eat a slice of watermelon and then spit out the seeds from machine-gun mouths. My favorite was the Spam cheer, which went, "Don't want no Treet, no Treet, don't want no meat, no meat, just give me that Spam!" And there were call-and-response interludes: "Boom-chick-a-boom . . ."

When the stars appeared, Ben brought out his guitar and taught us how the *Gilligan's Island* theme song shared a common meter with "House of the Rising Sun" and "Amazing Grace."

As the collective energy began to wind down, as the fire became coals, the songs turned sacred and melancholy. An old man sang "Loch Lomond."

I'd been watching from the back, leaning against the audio shed, taking it all in. I was no longer a participant, but removed, and this allowed me to see the objective wonder of it all, how hundreds of boys from all over Ohio could come together to shed their individuality and sync up as one, singing songs and shouting cheers. If you've ever been to a big, exciting pop concert, I suppose it's a similar feeling. There's a simple magic to it. And that's what we miss the most when it's over.

"Renner," someone whispered. I turned around. It was Trey. He was with Norman, who was waving me over. "Come with us." They jogged off down a path, two shadows in the tall bluegrass. I caught up to them as they crested a hill and made for Peninsula, the staff site behind the Wyandotte shower house. Trey ran to a big blue water barrel that was being used as a trash can and upended it, spilling its contents onto the ground.

"What're you doing?" I asked.

But Trey was already jogging away with it, back the way we'd come. "Don't worry," Norman said. "We'll put the trash back in a minute." He rummaged around in his tent and came out with a canoe paddle. Before I could ask, he started off after Trey.

Trey was halfway up the hill with the barrel on the ground, upside down. Norman was giggling.

"What—"

"Shh. Listen."

I listened. "Loch Lomond" was ending back at the Campfire. "'And the moon comin' out in the gloaming.'" Norman raised the paddle like a weapon.

Trey held up a hand. *Wait.*

The silence lengthened. A moment before it happened, I realized what we were doing. It felt a little like finding out that Santa Claus wasn't real.

Trey dropped his hand. *Now.*

Norman brought the paddle down on the barrel bottom. *BOOOOOOOM!* Then again and again in a familiar rhythm. *Bum-bum-bum-bah, bum-bum-bum-bah!* These were the mysterious, unseen drums that heralded the arrival of the Pipestone elder, an oar on a trash can. Norman continued, smacking the barrel louder and louder, faster and faster. Every time he hit the thing, I blinked involuntarily. I felt the percussion in my head. And then he stopped and silence rushed in.

From over the hill I heard the elder's voice, amplified by speakers. "In five days you are invited to take part in Pipestone," he said. His speech, like every other part of Pipestone, was ritualistic, unchanging through the years. I remembered how I'd listened to this speech with awe when I was eleven. Since then, I had earned four of the five degrees of Pipestone. If I completed the fifth-degree ceremony this summer, I would be able to participate in the ceremony itself.

I was apprehensive about Pipestone by then. The whole business about grown men painting their bodies red and wearing loincloths looked stranger the older I got. And the speech the chief of Pipestone had given to me and my fourth-degree graduates was odd to say the least. "Masturbation leads to curiosity," he'd told us in the dark woods at midnight. He warned us that touching ourselves could lead to immoral choices. "Beware of homosexual encounters," he'd said. "Homosexuals are immature. They are stuck in childhood forever. Leave your friendships with the same sex behind."

When the Pipestone elder finished his speech, we returned the barrel and cleaned up the garbage and then hurriedly joined the other counselors for this thing called Dire. So, remember how the Scouts are told to leave the Campfire quietly, with their arms folded, and to stay silent all the way back to camp to honor the chief of Pipestone? To enforce that, the staff would position themselves on trails throughout camp, and if they heard Scouts talking, they would remind them of their obligation. This was called Dire. I don't know why.

My friends and I took this as an invitation to scare the ever-loving shit out of some kids. Trey was particularly skilled at this. He would find an advantageous spot behind a tree along a dark part of the path; and when some Scout, thinking it was safe, thinking they were far enough from the Campfire to get away with it, would whisper to his friend, Trey would jump out from behind the tree like some malevolent spirit and say, "You are dishonoring the chief of Pipestone. Please continue in silence until you reach your campsite." From that point on, those kids would keep absolutely silent, assuming they were under constant surveillance.

I enjoyed this part of camp immensely and looked forward to it every Sunday.

By the time I started back toward CIT-ville, it was quite late. I took a path that led down steep steps cut into the side of the hill under the branches of old pines. The air was pungent with sap and cedar. I crossed the land bridge that cuts across Lake Donahey and continued on toward the dining hall at the top of the hill. As I approached, I heard a woman singing. At first, I thought it must be the radio, but as I got closer, I saw her silhouette through the curtains. A breeze blew the curtains aside and for a moment I saw a young woman on the stage. She had short, blond hair cut like a boy's and she wore a thin white dress that let light through in a way that set my pulse going. She was singing "Right Field," an old song popularized by Peter, Paul, and Mary, which was about a kid who doesn't play baseball very well because he daydreams during the games. I watched, mesmerized. I'd never had sex outside of that stuff that happened when I was eleven. But I was seventeen and it was on my mind all the time. I had girl-friends back home, and I'd gotten to second base earlier that year with a girl in a trailer park, when her mom wasn't home. It was terribly confusing, how I could be attracted to girls and boys. Maybe it was because I came from the outer rim of Ohio, from a farm town that remains twenty years behind any cultural shift, but I had never heard the term "bisexual." There was gay and there was straight, and if you were gay, you were a deviant. Simple as that.

So a part of me was relieved when my body quickened at the sight of this beautiful woman. I walked away before it got creepy. I took the narrow path into CIT-ville, anxious to be alone with my thoughts.

Once I got to my tent, I placed a flashlight on the pallet floor to illuminate the inside and was arranging my sleeping bag, when someone knocked on the center support pole. I pulled back the canvas flap. There was a man outside who looked familiar—he appeared to be in his midtwenties. It took me a moment to place him—he'd been the program director a year or two before, but I'd forgotten his name.

"Hi," he said. "I'm Mike Klingler. Are you the new CIT?"

I moved back so he could step inside. I introduced myself and shook his left hand in the Boy Scout way. "Not a CIT," I said. "I'm teaching First Aid. I wasn't here for setup because of a family vacation, so—"

"They stuck you here," he said. "That's fine. I just wanted to drop in and say hello. I'm the senior staff member in charge of CITs this year." Mike was thin and tall, with a high forehead. Friendly-looking. But I thought it was odd, even then, that he was in charge of CITs after being program director. That seemed like quite a demotion.

"Is there anyone else here right now?" I asked.

"Two others," he said. "Jared and Tim. Couple tents over."

"Cool."

"Well, if you need anything, I've got the tent up top." He meant the one under the big pine, the only tent with power down here.

"Thanks."

"Where are you from?"

"Uh, Ravenna. Sort of. You?"

"Beach City," he said. "You have elf ears."

"I do?"

"Yeah, they look like an elf's ears."

"Nobody ever told me that before."

"Are you a fifth year?"

"Pipestone? No. Fourth."

"Some speech, huh?"

"Yeah."

"Well, get some sleep. Reveille's at seven. You can help check knots. It's square knots in the morning. You can tie a square knot, right?"

"Yep."

"Good. Well, welcome to staff. Night, then."

He walked out of the tent, leaving me alone. I touched my ears, suddenly self-conscious.

I turned out the light, undressed to skivvies and climbed into my bag, old steel springs squeaking loudly underneath. The next day I found better accommodations. I didn't return to CIT-ville until after Mike was dead.

now

The Boy Scouts of America filed for bankruptcy on February 18, 2020, after mounting lawsuits from more than three hundred abused Scouts became too numerous to manage on a case-by-case level.

Jim Turley, then national chair for the Boy Scouts of America, penned an emotional letter to victims that was published on its website: *I am truly heartbroken that you were harmed during your time in Scouting and that you carry unfathomable pain.* And while he stated that much of the abuse had occurred due to the failings of local leaders, and not because of a systemic failure from the top, down, Turley did finally accept responsibility for the Boy Scouts of America itself: *I am sorry. I am devastated that there were times in the past when we failed the very children we were supposed to protect.* A monetary trust fund was being created, he said, to fairly compensate the victims.

Turley even asked more victims to come forward: *I encourage you and all victims to come forward and file claims so you can receive compensation from this Trust. We will provide clear notices about how to do so.*

And—oh, boy—the victims came forward. Over eighty-two thousand abused Scouts filed for compensation in the first few months.

I'm going to tell you about one.

Eric Palmer grew up in Chillicothe, Ohio. That's a blue-collar town south of Columbus, situated beside the Scioto River. The town derives its name from the Shawnee word *"Chala-ka-tha,"* which means "principal town," as it was the tribe's chief settlement until we forced them out and Anglicized their name. Chillicothe was a popular refuge for free Blacks before the Civil War, a major port of call for the

I like animals.

So . . . Ecology it is.

Underground Railroad. Mead Paper employed much of the town for decades. Eric's mother worked there for forty years.

When Eric was old enough, he joined the Boy Scout troop that met at Trinity United Methodist. Photographs from his first year show a happy, smiling child. A scoutmaster named Bill McKell took all that away. Bill was a friend of the family; Eric and Bill's younger sister were good friends. Bill was part of a powerful dynasty that owned the independent telephone company that serviced the region. He coached the Speech and Debate club at the local high school. In 1982, Bill was the director of Camp Logan Reservation, where many local troops went for summer camp. One day, when Eric was twelve, Bill asked the boy to ride out to Camp Logan with him.

When they got there, Eric realized that nobody else was at camp, which he thought was odd. There was a house there, which Bill had access to. He brought Eric into a room off the porch and they both sat on a couch. Bill started roughhousing with him, pretend-wrestling. But then Bill's countenance changed. He held Eric down with his body, pinning him against the couch. He rubbed a hand over the boy's crotch, then reached into his pants and digitally penetrated him.

Somehow Eric was able to wiggle out from underneath the man. He ran to another room and locked himself inside. Bill pleaded for him to come out. "I'm sorry if I upset you," he said. "We were just wrestling. Nothing happened. Please don't tell anybody."

After a while Eric came out and Bill drove him home and Eric didn't tell anybody for many years. But something fundamental had changed inside of him forever. He was no longer that smiley boy. His family asked him why he was so mopey all of the time. What nobody could see was the turmoil inside that twelve-year-old boy's mind. *Maybe it was my fault,* he wondered. *Maybe it was something normal that happens and isn't that big of a deal. Maybe nobody would believe me if I did tell someone.*

At school Eric's grades tanked. In college he found relief in alcohol, binge drinking to silence the negative thoughts that had followed him from Chillicothe.

Then, in 2010, the year he turned forty, Eric attended Bockfest, in the historic district of Cincy known as Over-the-Rhine. It's an annual spring tradition, a celebration centered around the tapping of bock beer, which was first brewed by German monks as a substitute for food during the Lenten fast. Be careful, though, if you choose to partake. Bock beer has a very high alcohol content. Eric and a friend attended in style that year and, in vino veritas, he told his story out loud for the first time. As men paraded down the streets dressed in monk robes and goat costumes, he let it all come out. And when it was over, he made a pact with his friend to find a therapist. When he got home, Eric told his wife. At first, she was upset. So much of what had confounded her about her husband suddenly made sense. They connected the dots together, how the childhood trauma had manifested as symptoms of PTSD; he was always jumpy, hypervigilant, overly protective of their children. And Eric followed through with his promise. He got professional help and he got on Lexapro.

The next person Eric told was his sister. She was a police officer in Chillicothe. And, of course, the first thing she did was confront Bill, who still lived in town. He ran from her. In short order an investigation was conducted. The police interviewed former Scouts, going back decades, and found twelve boys whom Bill had molested while serving as scoutmaster of Troop 5. Ah, but each crime was beyond the statute of limitations in the state of Ohio, where criminal charges must be brought within twenty years of a sexual assault. There was nothing the police could do . . . except to release the report of the investigation. Chillicothe is a small town, far from any major city, the kind of town that when you're in it, it feels like the whole world. And so when the news came out that everyone's favorite scoutmaster was a prolific pedophile, it was all anyone could talk about. If you lived there, it was likely you knew someone involved. Bill was promptly fired by the telephone company, where nepotism had awarded him the title of CEO. And then Bill did something nobody expected—he admitted to it.

My name is Bill McKell and I am a child molester, he posted on his personal Facebook profile. *Every twelve-step program begins with admis-sion. I have been one who abused teenage boys. As far as I am able to tell, it is a disease of the mind not unlike alcoholism or drug addiction. It is a sickness that can never be cured or healed, only recovered from. That being said, there is no excuse for what I have done.*

I attempted to speak with McKell directly, and even drove down to his place in southern Ohio, seeking further comment. His property has been turned into a campground, with several buildings, including a large communal cabin by a lake. It looks very much like a small Boy Scout retreat. But he disregarded notes stuck in doors and messages left by phone.

Even with the online confession, there was nothing the police could do, unless Bill did it again.

I met up with Eric at Nine Giant Brewing in Cincinnati a few days before Christmas. It's a gastropub with a selection of beers they brew on premises. Eric creates some of the beers himself when he's not practicing law. He's a lawyer now, labor law mostly, handling con-tract negotiations. He currently serves as the executive director of the American Association of University Professors. Sometimes he teaches a Legal Issues for Brewers class at Cincinnati State. He was fifty-two, with kids headed to college. He's got a trim white beard that com-pletes the kindly professor vibe. I ordered a craft beer infused with cucumber. It was the first alcoholic drink I'd had in some time. I know I'm not supposed to drink, but I'm not ordering soda water at a damn brewery. I finished it fast and ordered another.

"I want to go back," Eric said after some small talk.

"Go back where?" I asked.

"Camp Logan."

"Why?"

"Because of how society treats victims of sex abuse. There's always this belief that they might not be telling the truth. Those people can get to you, make you doubt yourself. But there's such a level of detail in my mind. So I want to go back and see that room where it happened. For validation. I think it might be healing for me."

When Bill posted his confession on Facebook, the backlash was immediate and fierce. If he was hoping for sympathy, it wasn't to be found on social media. He deleted the post within a day, but by then, the local newspapers had screenshots. It was a story that briefly traveled the world. Eric was surprised to find that he felt bad for Bill. But he's also uniquely aware of the damage that Bill inflicted on a generation of boys and how the fallout still ripples through time.

Take, for instance, the story of Dan Burris, another Scout from Chillicothe, who worked closely with Bill at Camp Logan for a time. In 2017, at the age of forty-six, Burris was sentenced to fourteen years in prison for raping and molesting two boys he met at a Boy Scout camp. One of his victims was eleven years old.

Molesting a child often creates an adult perpetrator, who continues the cycle.

"I wonder why Dan became that way and I didn't," Eric told me. He says it like someone who has witnessed an accident that killed some people, but not him. It's a there-but-for-the-grace-of-God kinda thing. If only this, if only that. The possibilities of another life.

So, yes, when the Boy Scouts of America announced monetary compensation, Eric applied. And, hey, the Boy Scouts are nothing if not pragmatic, so its website now includes a helpful calculator for sex abuse claims. You simply type in your state and the sort of abuse you suffered (penetration, oral) and it spits out the value of your claim. For instance, a blow job by a scoutmaster is worth nearly $500,000. Who knew?

Eric's claim is penetration. According to the calculator, since the abuse happened in Ohio, the most he could receive from the trust is $141,000. But if he'd been raped in a different state, he could get as much as $637,000. Why such disparity? You guessed it: the statute of limitations. According to current Ohio law, child sex abuse victims have until the age of thirty to sue for damages in civil court.

But Eric is a lawyer, a community organizer, and a clever

sonofabitch. He recognized that the law in Ohio needed to change and he was motivated to do what he could to help.

"And that's when I reached out to Jessica Miranda," he said.

————————

Jessica Miranda is the minority whip in the Ohio House of Representatives. She represents the 28th district, which serves the suburbs to the north of Cincinnati. She's passionate about gun reform and supporting public schools. And she's also a survivor of sexual assault. When she was a child, she was abused by an older relative whenever her single mother would go to work. At fifteen she was raped by a friend's older brother. In April 2022, Representative Miranda sat with reporters for the *Columbus Dispatch* and recounted her trauma in a raw interview about the need to change the archaic statutes of limitations in Ohio. The article identified the biggest roadblock to reform: her colleague, Republican majority leader, Bill Seitz.

Seitz hails from the red part of Cincinnati that feels more like Kentucky than Ohio and serves on the criminal and civil justice committees. By the time Representative Miranda's article came out, Seitz had earned a reputation for protecting the interest of institutions over sexual abuse victims. Case in point: In 2018, several wrestlers for the Ohio State University accused a former campus physician, Richard Strauss, of fondling and assaulting them during examinations (Strauss died by suicide in 2005). An investigation concluded that Strauss had abused at least 177 students during his tenure. Not for nothing, but some of these acts occurred when US congressman Jim Jordan was an assistant coach for the university, and the victims claim that he was aware of the abuse and chose to do nothing. When those students banded together to ask the Ohio legislature to extend the statute of limitations for sexual abuse so that they could receive appropriate compensation from OSU, Seitz told them he would not support it. He told one victim that he should have just reported the matter to the police when the abuse occurred. According to the *Dispatch,* "[Seitz] also said allowing survivors to sue institutions for negligence could

financially bleed organizations such as the Catholic church and the
Boy Scouts."

If the statute of limitations in Ohio was ever going to change, Representative Miranda needed to get Seitz on board. And that seemed
damn near impossible. And yet, it happened. Seitz coauthored a bill
that could negate the statute of limitations for sexual abuse by Boy
Scout leaders in Ohio. I had to find out how. So one winter morning,
I drove down to Columbus to ask her in person.

Representative Miranda's office is across the street from the statehouse, with a view of downtown. I sat on a couch across from her
and she told me the story about how she'd accidentally become the
loudest voice for reforming sexual abuse laws in Ohio.

"I was in a drive-thru when a reporter from the *Dispatch* called
me," she said. "I was distracted, trying to place my order, giving this
interview at the same time. She asked me why I was sponsoring a
bill to get rid of the statute of limitations for rape and to also extend
the statute of limitations for child abuse and I just spit out, 'Well,
it's more efficient for me. I'm a survivor of both.' And then we both
kind of realized what I'd just said. After a moment I told her I needed
to collect myself and I'd call her back. I had never said that out loud
before in my life, you know? I'm one of ninety-nine lawmakers in this
body. I didn't know if I wanted to be that vulnerable. So I called her
back and asked her not to print the story until I had time to process
and think about what I wanted to do. She was so kind. She let me
come to it, slowly."

Some months later, Representative Miranda called the reporter
back and said she was ready to talk about it all. The profile ran on the
front page of the newspaper. Copies of the paper are still displayed in
her office. "It was the greatest feeling of relief when I finally told my
story," she said.

The laws regarding sexual assault in Ohio are draconian. Society
has changed. The state's laws have not. For example, it's still legal in
the state of Ohio for a husband to drug and rape his wife. In recent
years bills have been written to close this loophole, but the bill always

stalls in committee. Why? For one, the old white men running the Prosecuting Attorneys Association are against it. They are afraid that women might lie about being victims as leverage in a divorce, according to an article in the *Ohio Capital Journal*.

So it was a surprise to everyone when Representative Miranda introduced legislation to alter sex laws in Ohio that was cosponsored by the most powerful Republican in the statehouse, Bill Seitz. House Bill 35, known as the Scout's Honor Law, would completely remove the statute of limitations for civil action based on a claim of childhood sexual abuse against an organization in bankruptcy for the next five years. Basically, it's a law just for the Boy Scout abuse victims to receive full compensation. But it's a significant step for victims' rights and an unexpected act of contrition from across the aisle.

"How'd you get Seitz?" I asked.

Representative Miranda smiled. "We ambushed him during a smoke break," she said. Here's how it went down. A man named Chris Graham reached out to her. Graham is a survivor of sex abuse as well. He was raped by a Catholic priest when he was fourteen and has been a vocal champion for victims of the Catholic Church for many years. He recognized the similarity between the Church scandal and the Boy Scout cases. He's the one who pointed out to Representative Miranda that they were dealing with a ticking clock. The Boy Scouts bankruptcy allows victims only one year to change statute of limitations laws in their home state to get the full monetary amount owed to them. They had to act fast for the two thousand Ohio men who had applied for compensation before the deadline.

Representative Miranda told Chris the best way to meet Seitz was to catch him on his routine smoke break. Every day at the same time, he would step outside the eastern doors and have a cigarette. So Chris rode down to Columbus with a man who was a victim of abuse within the Boy Scouts and ambushed Seitz on his break. To Chris's surprise, Seitz listened to the victim.

"All right," said Seitz. "Representative Miranda and I will talk."

"He gets it now," she said. "He understands that Ohio survivors will get the short end of the stick if we don't change the law."

"What's next for this bill?" I asked.

"We have a proponent hearing next Tuesday. We have victims of abuse within Scouting coming in to speak to the committee. There's nothing more powerful than survivors telling their stories."

"Next Tuesday?" I said. "Do you want one more voice?"

then

"Helmet Head!"

I was leaning on the Coke machine at the back of the scoutmaster's patio beside the dining hall, trying to wake up. It was a quarter after seven in the morning, by far the earliest I'd ever been electively awake in the summertime. Reveille had just played over the tinny loudspeakers across Seven Ranges. That was the call for each troop to send two Scouts to help set tables and to serve as waiters for breakfast. A few boys were already inside scooping bug juice into large pitchers from industrial-sized tanks.

"Helmet Head!" someone shouted again. I looked over to find a tall redheaded man with an apron standing at the door to the dining hall, looking at me. I didn't know who he was, but I could tell he was displeased.

"Me?"

"Do you see anyone else with hair that looks like a damned helmet?"

Back then, I put Dippity-do in my hair so my bangs could stick out a ways up front, like a visor. There was a show on TV I liked, *Parker Lewis Can't Lose*, and the lead actor had his hair the same way.

"Make yourself useful," he said. "Line up the mouth breathers and check their knots. Don't let me catch you napping again." And with that, he disappeared inside.

I walked around the dining hall to the main doors, where the first troops were arriving for breakfast. For dinner everyone wore Class-A uniform, the old brown and tan. But in the mornings the Scouts could wear shorts, jeans, T-shirts, whatever. Some looked like they'd slept in

I was leaning on the Coke machine at the
back of the scoutmaster's patio beside the
dining hall, trying to wake up.

their clothes. Hordes of sleepy-eyed teen boys approached like zombies, their hair sticking out at odd angles. Few had showered. Many would go the entire week without a shower, their only attempt at hygiene an afternoon swim in muddy Lake Donahey.

Trey and Norman came up the hill and together we lined up the troops. When the doors opened five minutes later, we stationed ourselves at the entrance and checked each boy's square knot as they passed by. I took it easy on them. If a boy accidentally looped the rope the wrong way and came up with a granny knot, I'd untie it for him and show him the proper twist. By the time everyone was inside, the dew on the grassy hill had begun to evaporate under the sun, steaming into the air.

Per tradition, everyone stood behind their seats, arms folded. Ben, the program director, walked through the mess and up to the stage at the front. He was dressed in Class-B, like me and the rest of the Seven Ranges staff—army-green Boy Scout shorts with belt and an official camp tee. As soon as everyone was quiet, Ben started the morning song.

When it was over, he yelled, "Seats!" and the Scouts yelled back, "Eats!" and everyone sat down. Once breakfast was served, the din of excited conversation and the *clink* and *clank* of utensils was overwhelming. I got used to it eventually. There's something almost comforting about it after a while. It comes with a feeling of community, of shared interests, of safety in numbers, of being part of a particular tribe. I'd always wanted to be a member of this tribe, to be on staff at Seven Ranges. It was almost too much to believe that it was finally happening.

After breakfast I walked to Admin to prepare for my First Aid class.

I had achieved the Life rank in Scouting, that's one step below Eagle. I had taken First Aid as a Tenderfoot, six years before, and most of what I'd learned was forgotten. But the merit badge pamphlet was easy enough to follow.

There's a separate entrance to the First Aid station on the side of

Admin. I knocked on the screen door, and after a moment my favorite counselor appeared on the other side. It was that magician who had performed at the Campfire my very first year at Seven Ranges, Lucas Taylor.

"Hey, buddy," he said, opening the door. "How ya been?"

The simple fact that he remembered me was enough to put a smile on my face. He was the closest thing to a real celebrity I'd ever met besides Dick Goddard, a weatherman in Cleveland, who autographed a photo for me at a parade when I was eight.

I entered the First Aid station, which was big enough for one hospital bed and a couple chairs. There were old-timey glass cabinets full of bandages and aspirin along one wall. I figured the worst thing that could happen at camp was food poisoning or a sprained wrist. I suppose there was the occasional broken bone, but they probably drove those kids straight to the closest hospital, over in Salem.

"I'm on staff, this year," I told Lucas. "I'm teaching First Aid."

"God help us," he quipped. "What do you need?"

"Do you have any splints?"

"Sure thing."

As he rummaged in the closet, I noticed there was another room in the back, its door open. There were two beds inside, one made up, the other just a mattress on a box spring.

"You live here?" I asked.

"Yessir. I've done enough tent camping. I've got my own shower, too, and it's always hot."

"Awesome."

"Here's your splints," he said, handing me a couple to practice with.

"Do you still do magic?"

"Oh, every now and then," Lucas said, and with a wave of his hand, he picked a playing card out of the air. Ace of Spades. Then, just as quickly, he made it disappear.

"Can you teach me how to do that?"

"A magician never reveals his secrets," he said, but he did it with a smile.

Lucas also served as camp chaplain that summer. I think his mother was a minister or something, because he liked to joke that his congregation at Seven Ranges was larger than hers back home. His sermons were short and always included several songs. When he was at the pulpit, he wore a guitar slung around his neck. Magic, music, and jokes. Lucas was made for being a camp counselor and he was the best of the bunch. I don't want you to read further expecting him to do something bad and that all of this is foreshadowing. Lucas was the ideal Boy Scout and I don't expect there were many like him. And even if he no longer returns my calls, I still love him like a brother. He was the first one to figure out what was going on with Tommy. He was the one who spoke to the police. But that comes later.

Around nine o'clock, a dozen Scouts gathered around a picnic table outside to learn First Aid. I followed the instruction booklet and taught them how to recognize when someone was in shock, which could happen not just with a visible injury, but also with types of poisoning. I showed them drawings of black widow spiders and scorpions so they could identify venomous bugs (though it's far too cold for scorpions to survive in Ohio). Then we took turns putting splints on each other.

That morning group was my favorite. The boys were rested and fed and excited for the day; by the time class was over, the sun had warmed the world and the air was pungent with pine and prairie flowers. At the height of summer in the Ohio country, the trees and grasses are so lush that it feels as if nature owns the world again and could swallow everything up if given another day, and all of humanity would be only a memory, a bad dream. It was green everywhere, obscenely verdant. Scary almost. We lived inside it.

After dinner that night I walked back to Peninsula with Norman and Trey and hung out in their tent with a couple older staffers. Their place was arranged for hosting, with the beds to either side and a nice carpet and a couple chairs in the middle. Trey had shipped a dresser into camp, which stood in the back, and there was soft lighting like a den. A cheap stereo played cassette tapes; Trey was deep into Nirvana at the time.

"Do you guys watch *The X-Files?*" I asked.

"I watch Gillian Anderson," said Norman with a grin.

That year I was obsessed with *The X-Files*. Season Two had just ended on a cliffhanger. Agent Fox Mulder had gone into a boxcar full of dead aliens and the Cigarette Smoking Man had maybe killed him, blown him up. "Have you ever seen a real UFO?" I asked.

"I've seen Uranus," said Trey.

"Funny," I said. "But seriously, I saw something once. My dad and I, we were coming back from soccer practice and there were these four lights in the sky coming toward us in a straight line, one behind the other. And as soon as they got over the top of us, they disappeared, like they went into some invisible mothership or something."

"Far out," said Trey. He reached into the drawer of his dresser and came out with a pack of cigarettes. He stuck one in his mouth and put the rest back. "I like a smoke after dinner," he said. "Anybody else?" He lit the cigarette with a cheap, gas station lighter, took a drag, and then handed it to me.

I contemplated my next move. My stepmother smoked two packs of Virginia Slims every single day. Sometimes I'd sneak a pack out of her purse and throw them in the trash just to piss her off. One more petty win in our ongoing cold war. Until that moment I had regarded smoking with disgust, through simple association. But here was Trey offering me a cigarette and my body got tingly with electricity, because isn't sharing a smoke something like a kiss?

I took the cigarette from Trey's fingers and placed it between my lips. I took a pull and then passed it back.

"What was that?" asked Trey.

"What?"

"That's not smoking. You just took it in your mouth and blew it out."

"What are you supposed to do?"

"Watch." Trey took a drag and opened his mouth so I could see the smoke in there. Then he inhaled and the smoke disappeared into his lungs. He exhaled, then passed the cigarette back. "Take the smoke into your mouth and then breathe in."

I took another pull. Then I inhaled deeply. And holy fucking shit, I swear I could feel each individual cilium in my lungs catching fire like a forest ignited by pyroclastic debris after a volcanic eruption. It hurt so much. I coughed uncontrollably and handed it back to Trey before stumbling out of the tent, into the night. I could hear the other guys inside laughing loudly as if it was the funniest goddamn thing they'd ever seen. I was just regaining my breath when I felt a hand on my back. It was Trey. He was trying to stifle a laugh, but he was also concerned.

"I'm an asshole," he said. "Sorry about that. Come back inside."

When we returned, the conversation turned to an incident that had happened at Seven Ranges in 1993, two years before—the fire at the old Trading Post. I was at camp that week, as a Scout, and I remember the amber light reflecting off the low clouds over where the Trading Post stood. The oxygen canisters they used for soda had exploded with high-pitched whistles, shooting into the sky like fireworks. Some staffers had formed a fire brigade to keep it contained. They were lucky it didn't burn the whole camp down. They were lucky nobody died.

Word among the staff was that it was arson. And if it was arson, it had to be someone on staff that year. It couldn't have been a Scout, since the sabotage had happened inside the locked building. And only a few staff members had access to Trading Post keys. But nobody was ever arrested.

"Who do you think it was?" asked Trey.

Norman shrugged. "It was a weird year," he said. "It was a new crew. No more Dave Wagner. None of the old guys. Mike Klingler was program director."

Around nine o'clock, a dozen Scouts

gathered around a picnic table outside

to learn First Aid.

"How did he go from program director to babysitting CITs?" I asked.

"Dunno."

"Does anyone remember the year before that, when someone tortured Wagner's cat?" I asked. When I was met with blank stares, I told them the story. I remembered it clearly because it was the one time I'd ever seen Dave Wagner's confidence shaken. He came into the dining hall during lunch one day and from the stage addressed the gathered Scouts.

"I saw something today I never thought I'd see at this camp," he said. "I saw cruelty. There's a cat that lives here. She's an outside cat, but she comes up around back for food at night and we've gotten to love her like any other pet. This morning I found her wrapped in duct tape. I had to rush her to the vet and they're working on her right now, trying to carefully cut off all the tape. I actually don't know if she will live. Someone here, someone at camp this week, did this. And I can't understand why. I cannot understand that level of cruelty. I . . ." Dave Wagner trailed off, then just walked offstage and disappeared into the kitchen.

"Did he find out who did it?" Norman asked.

"Not as far as I know. But I've heard that people who play with fire are often cruel to animals, too. It's part of something called 'the Macdonald triad.'" I'd read that in a book about serial killers. Human predators often share three similar traits: arson, bed-wetting, and cruelty to animals.

"Well, the old crew is back this year," Norman said. "So, if there really was a psycho on staff, they're here with us."

We all slowly considered one another. Then Trey grabbed Norman like he was going to kiss him, passionately, but then he moved his hand over Norman's mouth at the last moment to block his lips. He pantomimed making out with him and we all laughed, while Norman twisted out from under his grip. That broke the tension in the room.

"Next time brush your teeth," said Norman.

The tent flaps opened then and a seventeen-year-old boy named

Tommy Hostetler came in swinging a six-pack. "Anyone want a cold beer?" he asked. We all did, of course. Tommy was very particular about many things, including his root beer. It was IBC, which only came in bottles with the tops you had to pry off with a church key, like a real beer. He had a tiny fridge in his tent for his bottles, which he shared with whoever came to visit him. He ran the FROG program that summer, which was for the youngest of Scouts to learn about nature and crafts. They met each morning on the cement foundation of the old Trading Post, where someone had painted a giant green lily pad.

Tommy was the sort of boy who always looked happy. He was always smiling, the kind of smile that reached into your soul and made you smile too.

Some theoretical physicists believe that time is an illusion, that everything is happening right now and our perception of the passage of time is all a big misunderstanding. They believe that nothing separates the past from the present, that if only we could access some higher dimension we might travel back and forth on a whim, the way three-dimensional objects roll over a two-dimensional plane.

But if there's a way to change the past, I haven't found it. All I can do is watch this all play out again in the pages of this book. My greatest fear is that by putting these stories down, it cements them into reality, somehow, unchangeable forever. Please don't let that be true. Because I'd very much like to save Tommy.

I was walking back to my tent that night after the root beers were finished when I noticed a light on in the First Aid office. I could see figures moving around in there. And after a moment I heard Lucas shouting.

I jogged over and opened the door.

"Renner, thank God!" said Lucas.

There was a young man lying on the bed behind him. His skin had turned gray and he was gasping for breath. Another Scout, a friend from the same troop, stood beside this boy, eyes wide with shock.

"What happened?" I asked.

"This knucklehead got some wood covered in poison ivy and put it on their campfire."

"We didn't know it was poison ivy," said the Scout standing beside him.

"He got the smoke in his lungs."

"Oh, shit," I said.

"I need you to go wake up his scoutmaster," said Lucas. "They're over in Chippewa. I have to wait for the ambulance. Here, take my car." He handed me his keys. "It's the blue Escort in the parking lot. Pick up his scoutmaster and bring him back."

"Got it," I said. I ran outside at a sprint and found Lucas's Escort not far away. I got behind the wheel, closed the door, and that's when I realized his car was a stick shift. Also I did not have my license, even though I was seventeen. Why? Because I had failed maneuverability five times in an automatic.

But, really, how hard could it be? I said a short prayer and started the car.

now

I did not comprehend that I was abused as a child until I was forty years old. See, when you're the victim of abuse at a very young age, you assume it's typical behavior. You're still learning about the world, building representative models of it in your mind. *This too must be a part of normal life,* you think. To finally recognize the abuse, it sometimes takes an outside perspective to show it to you. It was a trip to the doctor's office that did it for me.

I had this recurring pain in my left ear. It came and went with the weather. Sometimes it was just a dull presence, an annoyance in the background, but other days the pain was so unbearable, I couldn't think of anything else. To me, it felt like the locus of the pain was a millimeter inside my ear canal. It felt like maybe a splinter had gone deep into the skin there. So I used tiny mirrors and tweezers to probe inside, but I never could find anything. This went on for several years, until one day it got so bad that I made an appointment to see my doctor.

Dr. Palmer is young man who looks a bit like Matthew Morrison and always asks me about my next book. Good guy. I told him about my ear and he looked inside and found nothing again.

"I'm not crazy," I said. "It really hurts."

"Hmm," he said. "I had a friend once who broke his jaw, and afterward, he said his ear hurt more than anything else. There are nerves that run along the jaw to the ear. Could be your jaw."

"I don't think it's my jaw," I said.

"Can I check?"

"Sure."

But if there's a way to change the past,

I haven't found it.

He reached out with his right hand and touched my left cheek. When he made contact, pain exploded in my head, reaching out like branches of lightning from my jaw, around my ear, and into my temple. I yelped in a very undignified way.

"You've got a fracture right here," he said. "Did somebody hit you when you were a little kid?"

"No," I said. "I got into a couple fights in school, but nothing that serious."

"I don't mean fights with other kids. I'm asking, did somebody hit you when you were little?"

I started to say, "No," but then I remembered. Yes, somebody had hit me when I was little. Somebody hit me a lot. Right there, where my jaw was fractured. Until that moment I'd never identified as a victim of abuse. I'd always assumed that this sort of thing was common in families. Parents hit their children with a closed fist and you dealt with it. But I didn't know anyone else who was hit so hard they fractured a jaw. That's what made me finally realize the punishments my stepmother subjected me to were physical assaults. Her reactions to my childish behavior had been neither tempered nor entirely sane.

"Well, shit," I said.

It's the sort of random realization that sends a person into therapy. Luckily, I have a professional support team I've fostered over the years. I have my regular psychologist, Dr. Deb, whom I see for an hour, every other week. And I have a psychiatrist who prescribes me antianxiety and antidepression medication (Citalopram, Buspirone), and when I meet with him, I have a session with his personal therapist, too.

There was a time, a few years ago, when I couldn't stop catastrophizing. From the moment I woke until the time I drank myself to sleep at night, my mind was nothing but a swirl of anxious thoughts about my future and depressive thoughts about my past. It was the usual imposter syndrome stuff, exacerbated by social media. It was more than bad book reviews, though. There was one guy who was so upset with my last book that he followed my family to the Outer

Banks and left a threatening note on the steps of our vacation rental. I was an asshole for writing about the case, they said. I was a disgusting reporter, out to make money off Maura Murray's disappearance.

The stress of being targeted by online trolls was an ever-constant drain and eventually I began to see myself the way they saw me. I started to believe them. I lost my appetite and shed sixty pounds in two months. I felt like the guy in *Thinner,* but I swear I never ran over an old gypsy woman. All I did was write a couple true crime books. The scary thing about being an adult is that you can legitimately lose control of your mind if you're not careful. And it happens quickly. I came to realize that there was one surefire way to quiet all those negative thoughts: There's a bridge in Akron that crosses over the Cuyahoga River and it's high enough that you don't run the risk of waking up in the hospital, paralyzed. Anyway, that's the moment I made an appointment with Dr. Deb.

Her office is not far from my house. She mostly sees children. She's a fan of harm reduction as opposed to abstinence for things like alcohol. She doesn't mind that I smoke pot.

"What do you want out of this?" she asked me the first time we met.

"I want to smile again," I said.

We talked about my stepmother. We talked about my sexual awakening at summer camp when I was eleven. She made me aware of the bad habits I'd slipped into that were keeping me from joy. For example, my morning routine was sabotaging my mood for the entire day. I'd gotten into the habit of checking social media as soon as I woke up. What were the haters saying about me today? Had someone created a fake Facebook fan page full of unflattering pictures of me? Had a blogger posted my wife's cell phone number again? All those things really did happen. I assumed they would happen again, forever, and I was in a hypervigilant mode all day, constantly performing a damage assessment of my reputation.

Dr. Deb helped me organize a better routine. No checking social media before I showered and had breakfast, until I'd gotten the kids off to school. The first few days were difficult; I felt the pull of my phone, the need to know if I was being maligned. But that short delay eventually allowed me to see the futility of what I'd been doing for years. Why the hell should I care what someone I have never met thinks of me? What business is it of mine? And what did the knowing accomplish, other than making a day crummy the moment it began?

One day Dr. Deb wrote something on a scrap of paper and handed it to me: *There is no light without darkness and no psychic wholeness without imperfection.* I stuck it on the wall above my office desk. It's still there.

At some point I discovered Alan Watts and, wow, if you don't know about him, do yourself a favor and put his name into YouTube or TikTok. He was this beatnik hippy philosopher from England who settled in Northern California in the '60s. His lectures on existentialism, Buddhism, and the Tao were broadcast on public radio in San Francisco for years after his death in 1973. He experimented with psychedelics while writing essays like "The New Alchemy." The things he said gave me a better perspective on reality.

"Man suffers only because he takes seriously what the gods made for fun," Watts said.

Watts had a grand idea about what we are and why we are here. He believed that we are the aperture through which the universe is looking at and exploring itself, that we are all the same thing, the same single consciousness. He believed that the "self," our ego, our singular identity, is only a temporary illusion.

Humans have this weird, innate belief that we are separate from everything else on Earth. We tend to believe there's something magical about being human, that we must be the only creatures with self-awareness and the ability to use our imagination. But what are we really, other than the natural conclusion of an evolutionary process that favored these things? Our universe tends toward consciousness. Anyone who has a dog understands that our best friends have a little consciousness in them, too. They dream and they feel shame. Same for dolphins and octopuses and ravens and great apes. We've just got more consciousness. And what is it doing for us? What is the reason for it, if not to analyze and understand the universe around us? We are beings created by the natural process of the universe and it seems like we're made to look back at it and figure it out.

Don't try to understand what Watts is saying all at once. Like, let it sit for a bit in the back of your mind. Come around to it again when you're falling asleep at night or when you're high with your friends.

Anyhow, what I've found is that thinking about this stuff dissolves my anxiety and depression. Or at least it reduces the severity. Because, like Watts, I've come to realize that what I see as my "self" is a misunderstanding. We are all connected and we really are the same big thing. So we don't have to feel pain when being maligned. Who are the haters maligning but themselves? How sad for them for not knowing this.

I try to keep this idea in mind when I get mad at someone. It's helpful to imagine that they're simply another extension of the "I" of the "me" of the "us," and I shouldn't be mean to them because why on Earth would I be mean to me? It doesn't work all the time. It especially doesn't work in the school pickup line.

When I think of Linda, I imagine my stepmother as a piece of the universe that didn't ever understand that we're all in this together. Nobody taught her this. And she never found it out on her own. She died of a sudden heart attack at age fifty while she was hosing out bugs from the grille of her minivan outside her double-wide. Dead before she hit the ground. But when I think of Linda, I picture her as an old woman who looks forward to my visits and I sit with her and feed her, because she can't feed herself anymore, and I read to her the Stephen King books she brought into the house and left for me to find.

I know that she abused me. I realize that now. And that's a powerful thing. It's when you can start forgiving, I think.

The thing that happened with Craig at Seven Ranges when I was eleven remains less clear. Would you call it abuse? When I was eleven years old, could I have given consent to another child? I don't blame Craig. I blame whoever introduced him to sex at that confusing age. Maybe one day I'll ask him who it was.

On the last day of February 2023, I drove to the statehouse in Columbus to witness several men tell tales of their abuse at the hands of scoutmasters, proponent testimony for House Bill 35, also known as the Scout's Honor Law. If it passes, victims in Ohio will be eligible for full compensation from the Boy Scouts of America bankruptcy. I arrived early, which was good because I got lost in the legislature building. There's a central rotunda and long halls at the points of the compass, but every hall looks like the other and each hall leads to more halls and then down sets of stairs that lead to more rooms and walkways. It's a big maze. I found a room in the basement where you could buy a cup of coffee and pay for it by placing money into a box. There were no employees present. It was on the honor system. Somehow that's very Ohio.

The hearing was held in the Taft room in front of the committee for civil and criminal justice. Eric Palmer was present, along with Chris Graham and a couple other men who'd driven in to give testimony. I recognized one man as the owner of a restaurant near my house. He was raped by his scoutmaster at least a hundred times between 1967 and 1969. This has been going on for so long. When it was his turn to speak, Chris read the man's prepared statement for him. He could only stand next to Chris, too emotional to speak, even after fifty-plus years.

The next witness was older still. "My name is Steve and I am a seventy-year-old BSA sexual abuse survivor," he began. "In July 2020, my husband came in from the garage to find me collapsed and sobbing on the family room floor. I was watching television and saw an advertisement for the Boy Scouts of America sexual lawsuit. All the memories I had suppressed for fifty-five years came flooding back to me and I was inconsolable for several days."

He finally told his partner the truth: An assistant scoutmaster had abused him for years, beginning in 1963, when he was ten. The abuse occurred at Camp Falling Rock in Licking County. It continued until he was sixteen, when he finally left the Scouts for good.

Eric Palmer spoke then. He told his story about Bill McKell and how the abuse had been a heavy shadow on his life for so many years. "The tentacles of a child sexual abuser don't just strangle the emotions of the kid they prey upon, they have lifelong effects," he said. "They affect friendships and trust, relationships and intimacy. They impair the ability to be an affectionate and compassionate parent. They caused me to be less than fully open and honest with my wife, up until the past several years; with my parents, who I feared would blame themselves or take angry, even aggressive action against the Scout leader who did it."

Near the end of his testimony, Eric said something profound. "As you can see here today, we survivors of sexual abuse in the Boy Scouts are forming a new brotherhood in place of the one that the Boy Scouts knowingly took from us as kids," he said. "It's a brotherhood of which we didn't ask to be a part, but was forced upon us in a very real, physical, and violent sense. Those here today are just the tip of the iceberg."

Eventually they called my name and I stepped to the podium with my typed statement clasped in one hand. "'My name is James Renner. I am speaking today in support of House Bill 35.'" I told them about everything that happened with Mike Klingler that summer. And I told them about the ritual of Pipestone, its homophobic and creepy speeches, and how that summer ended for me and my friends.

"'In 1995, a Pipestone leader took me and three other teenage boys into a sweat lodge. He told us to strip naked . . .'"

then

The night was quiet at Seven Ranges for a moment more. The robins had nested in the trees. Lake Donahey was still, its calm surface reflecting the Big Dipper. And then, from the direction of Admin, came the sound of a manual transmission crying for help.

"Motherfucker!" I yelled, pumping the clutch as I manhandled the gearshift. The Escort lurched forward, sputtered, died. "Come on!" I shouted. I managed to get her into first gear this time and decided to drive slowly and to not attempt second. The stereo blasted REM's "It's the End of the World as We Know It." I clicked off the sound and felt around for the headlights. Found them. But nobody else was on the gravel road this late.

It took me ten minutes to reach Chippewa. I parked the car and ran down the path to a circle of army tents I could barely see in the darkness. I knocked on the central support pole of the first one. "Hello?" I said.

A bleary-eyed Scout lifted the flap.

"Where's your scoutmaster?" I asked.

He pointed to a tent across the way. I ran over, knocked again. There was the sound of metal springs and then a large man appeared.

"We have a couple of your boys at First Aid. One's gonna have to go to the hospital. He's having trouble breathing. Can you come?"

"Yes, yes," he said, gathering a flannel shirt, which he buttoned as he walked. He went to the tent beside his, where he woke the assistant scoutmaster before following me back to the Escort.

"Can you, um, drive a stick?" I asked. Of course, he could. He got us back to Admin as the ambulance pulled into the lot. While Lucas

The night was quiet at Seven Ranges for

a moment more. The robins

had nested in the trees.

got the scoutmaster up to speed, I watched the paramedics load the boy onto a stretcher and then into the vehicle. They put an oxygen mask on him right away. Finally the scoutmaster hopped in the back, the doors closed, and away they went. After the other boy went back to his troop, Lucas collapsed into a chair.

"Wow," he said. "That was a first."

"Is he going to be okay?" I asked.

"He responded to the Benadryl I gave him. He'll be all right, but for a minute there . . . For a minute I wasn't sure. He turned blue, you know? Not the best way to start the summer. Bad omen."

"Seems like you could use an assistant up here at night for stuff like that," I said.

He smiled. "You think so?"

"I mean, you have an extra bed, and if something bad happens, you need someone to go get their leader, right?"

"You just want a hot shower and an inside toilet."

"They stuck me in CIT-ville. There's nobody my age down there."

Lucas nodded. "Take the bed."

And that's how the least experienced staffer at Seven Ranges ended up moving into Admin, the coziest of accommodations.

I quickly fell into a new routine. In the mornings I taught First Aid to young Scouts and in the afternoons I slung slushies at the Trading Post with Trey and Norman. We snuck Airheads when Mark, our boss, wasn't looking. We all tormented Mark in our own petty ways, but Trey turned it into an art form. He'd hide stock so that Mark had to order hundreds of new Boy Scout pins from the main office, and the day before they arrived, Trey would put the pins back. It annoyed Mark greatly, but he was too nice to do anything about it. Harmless pranks, after all, are tradition at any summer camp. I enjoyed watching the skits the staff performed at each meal. Since I had missed that first planning week, I was not in the skits myself. That was fine by me. I enjoyed watching from the peanut gallery.

My favorite performance happened every Wednesday at lunch. That's when Becky Einhorn sang "Right Field."

Becky was the girl from the window—the one I'd seen practicing that first night at camp. After the plates were cleared, she strolled into the dining hall with a baseball cap covering her short hair. She wore a simple pickup league jersey, the kind with the piping on the sleeves, a glove on her left hand. She bobbed between the long tables of Scouts, singing that song, never making eye contact, lost in her own space. I tell you every boy watched silently. Nobody stirred. Nobody made a joke to interrupt the moment. The room was absolutely quiet except for her voice. We were mesmerized in the literal sense. Once a week she owned that room for three minutes and change. And then a little flourish at the end. There was a string tied to a coffee can hidden in the rafters and at the part of the song where the underdog makes the play, Ben would pull on it and a baseball would tumble out and she would catch it.

I found out later that Becky was engaged to be married to Ben. They'd come to camp as a couple (they were both in their midtwenties). But every Wednesday at lunch, I got to see her and I got to witness five hundred Scouts fall in love with her in an instant.

After lunch I went down into CIT-ville to collect my gear to bring back to Admin. A couple CITs had moved into the other tents, but it was still mostly empty and the site felt abandoned like an ancient ruin of something hidden in the pines. As I started for Admin, Klingler came out of his tent.

"Renner," he said. "C'mere a minute."

I walked over and he motioned for me to come into his tent. He kept the flaps rolled up and tied to allow for a breeze, and we could see out to the path where Scouts were walking back to their campsites for siesta, a half hour of quiet before Waterfront opened. Klingler motioned for me to sit on his bed, which was tidy and made-up. He sat on a wooden crate across from me.

"Where are you sleeping?" he asked.

"I'm at Admin, with Lucas."

"Nice. Well, you're welcome back anytime."

"Thank you."

"What troop are you from?"

"Five-five-eight."

"Great Trail Council."

"That's right."

"I don't think we've ever had someone from 558 on staff."

"I love camp," I said. "I remember the summer you were program director."

Something passed behind his eyes. A thought or something. But he kept his smile. "That was a rough summer," he said.

"My troop was here when the Trading Post burned down."

"Man, that was a scary night. I'm glad nobody got hurt."

"What do you think happened?"

"Probably squirrels chewing on the wiring. They live in the pines."

"I heard they found duct tape or something that kept the sprinklers from going off."

"Who told you that?"

I shrugged. "I can't remember. But if it's true, wouldn't it have had to be someone on staff?"

"Why are you so interested in the old Trading Post?"

"I mean, it's kind of a mystery, isn't it? Like an unsolved mystery at Seven Ranges."

"Oh, man, there's so many mysteries at camp. Geez. Maybe some night I'll tell you some stories that'll make you keep the lights on."

"Deal," I said. I stood, ready to leave. As I stepped down to the floor of pine needles, I turned back. "How come you decided to not be program director after that summer?"

"Too much stress," he said. "Besides, I like this job. Looking after the counselors-in-training. They're still too young to be jaded. I'm an elementary teacher back home in Beach City."

"Oh, good," I said.

"Have a good one, Renner. Come back anytime."

Later that night I filled Trey and Norman in on this latest development in my investigation.

"Do you think he told you the truth?" asked Norman.

"I don't know," I replied. "The way he talked about it was weird, but he was in charge of camp that summer. In charge of the program, at least. Why would he want to burn down the Trading Post?"

"I heard some of the Trading Post staff tied him to a picnic table," said Trey. "You know, as a joke. So maybe it was payback." I know we picked on Mark, our manager, but I could never picture going so far as to tie him to a table.

"He didn't say anything about that."

"Well, I know he pissed a lot of people off that summer," Norman added. "He was bangin' Stan Carson's sister. She worked in the kitchen that year. Klingler had sex with her and told everyone she had hairy nipples and Stan flipped out."

"Huh."

"Yeah, it was a whole thing."

"Then why did he come back?" I asked. "I mean, if he was pissed off enough to burn it down, why come back?"

Of course, nobody had an answer.

Later that night Norman brought us around to the deck behind the dining hall, where the older staffers hung out after meals. To get there you had to cut through the kitchen and take a set of narrow stairs leading up to the second floor. The rule at Seven Ranges was that you could smoke out back, but only if you were eighteen. Scooter, the camp director, was usually back there holding court. It was a mature clique, the top echelon of camp, where all the big decisions were made. I wondered how Norman had earned enough cred to get us in.

There were about five or six staff members when we arrived. Everyone knew Norman and Trey, already, so Norman introduced me to the group.

"I hear they call you Helmet Head," said Scooter when I stepped onto the deck.

"They're just jealous of my hair," I replied, running my fingers across the shelf of hair above my eyes. Scooter's hair was already thinning.

"You look like Parker Lewis."

I looked over to find a young woman in a Class-A Boy Scout uniform. She was smoking a long cigarette, but didn't appear to be old enough to smoke. And she had this casual, sardonic smile, like she was in on a joke that the rest of us didn't understand. She leaned on the railing across from Scooter like she owned it.

"It's a good show," I said.

"Yeah, if you're straight-edge."

In the mid-1990s you were either straight-edge or alternative. I considered myself alternative, but I also pegged my acid-washed jeans.

"Kidding," she said. "What's your real name?"

"James."

She came over and shook my hand. "I'm Lauren," she said. "I'm over at Ecology."

"Cool," I said. The rest of the group were lost in other conversations, so I moved closer to Lauren. "How long have you been on staff?"

"This is my first year."

"Were you a Scout?" I knew some troops were starting to let girls in, but I'd never met one.

"No," she said with a laugh. "All my friends are boys and I got tired of losing them every summer. I'm from Dover, with Dan Arbor and Josh Riggenbacher. Josh said I should just come to camp with them. And I like animals. So . . . Ecology it is." She took a long drag on her Virginia Slim.

"How do you like it so far?"

"An assistant scoutmaster proposed to me today, so there's that. I've got that going for me. But listen to this bullshit. They won't let me take Pipestone."

"Who won't?"

"The Pipestone chief or something. Said it wasn't made for girls. But you know, I'm in charge of the Blacksnake Challenge and he doesn't have any problem with that."

The Blacksnake Challenge was an old tradition at Seven Ranges. If a Scout happened upon a blacksnake (and they were everywhere, sunning themselves on the trails on hot days), they could take it to

Ecology and someone like Lauren would measure it and then put it in an aquarium. Whoever captured the longest snake got a prize at the end of the week.

"What does the Blacksnake Challenge have to do with Pipestone?" I asked her.

"You don't know?"

I shook my head.

"They use them in the ceremonies. The Indians wave them around in front of the kids. They dance around with them while they're chanting. But that's only if we have live ones in the aquariums at the end of the week."

"That's creepy."

"No shit," said Lauren. "But the chief is worried that if I take Pipestone, his loincloth will shift and I'll accidentally see his dick. It's like, *hello,* I work at a Boy Scout camp. There isn't a day that goes by I don't accidentally see a dick."

My face turned red. This was not a conversation I'd ever had with a girl.

"You're sweet," she said. "I didn't mean to embarrass you."

We shot the shit for a while, and sometime around eleven, Trey, Norman, and I said our goodbyes and walked around to the loading docks, where two industrial refrigerators hummed loudly. The fridges were stocked with leftovers. We made sandwiches out of French toast and sausage and ate them sitting down with our feet dangling over the edge of the loading dock. After a moment the overhead light clicked on and that tall redheaded chef came out.

"Helmet Head!" he shouted. "You stealin' my food?"

I jumped and stumbled over an answer. But Norman just laughed.

"Go to bed, Cookie," he said.

"Don't be a smart-ass," the cook said. "It's late. You boys need some sleep. Take your snacks and hit the bricks."

"Thanks, uh, Mr. . . ."

"It's Ronald."

"Mr. Ronald."

"No. Not Mr. nothing. Jesus Christ, Helmet Head's not the bright-est bulb in the pack, is he?"

"I . . ."

"Back to your bunk, Tenderfoot."

I walked with Trey and Norman a bit before parting ways and heading back to Admin. Lucas wasn't there, so I let myself in with the key he'd given me. I took a long, hot shower, changed into shorts and a T-shirt, and climbed into bed. At home I always felt anxious (Dr. Deb would later explain to me how abused kids learn to stay in fight-or-flight mode at all times, in case they need to make an escape). But here at camp I felt safe. Safer than I ever remembered feeling. It was another world, self-contained, existing outside of fear and anger. At camp there was no past. It was only always now.

On Friday that first week, I got to act in a couple skits at a Camp-fire for the small group of boys who stayed behind while everyone else crossed the road to participate in Pipestone. We did this one sketch called "How Indians Tell Time," in which Trey, Norman, and I dressed as Native Americans and slowly marched from one side of the stage to the other while chanting in pidgin Cherokee until another staffer, offstage, yelled, "Shut up! It's four o'clock in the morning!"

When the sun set, the leftover Scouts returned to their camp-sites, and Trey, Norman, and I hung out in Tommy's tent and drank IBC root beer and discussed the highlights of Week One.

"Renner, you missed the squid," Norman said with a grin.

"The squid?"

"Down at Waterfront. That lady scoutmaster from Troop 530 came down and her pubes were sticking out the bottom of her swimsuit—"

"Like tentacles," Trey finished.

"Guys," said Tommy. "C'mon. Gross."

"Well, it's true," said Trey.

Thus began an in-depth discussion on the subject of "bush." Whether we had ever seen it firsthand (no, only glimpses in porno mags found along creek beds or hidden in attic rafters) and whether a woman having hair down there was sexy. This was a few years before online sex sites made everybody start shaving. Tommy was visibly uncomfortable, and after a while we had to talk about something else.

By the time I returned to Admin that night, the first-year Pipestone candidates were just returning from the woods on the other side of the road, young boys with wide eyes, walking in silence. For the first time I could see them from the outside, not as one of them, but as (almost) an adult. And what I saw made me uneasy. It was the last night of what should be a magical week of camp and these boys looked like they'd returned from some battle, shell-shocked.

Parent pickup was at 11 a.m. on Saturday. After a breakfast of sausage gravy and biscuits, I walked through the kitchen and up the stairs to the staff deck, hoping to find Lauren. I liked talking to her. It wasn't like talking to a girl at school. She was more like one of the guys. And I guess she was the first girl I was actually friends with, the way I was friends with other boys. But she wasn't there. The only person on the deck at that time was a young staffer named Rick May. He sat at the picnic table, smoking a giant cigar.

"Renner," he said. "How are you this fine day?"

"I'm good, Rick. What's with the stogie?"

"I'm celebrating."

"Celebrating what?"

"My home troop is here this week, did you know?"

"No."

"Yeah. And I finally told Scooter that my scoutmaster likes to diddle kids. So right now, they're escorting him out of camp. When I finish this cigar, I'm going to go home, and with any luck he'll be arrested before the end of the day."

I never saw Rick again.

now

Officially, the Boy Scouts of America does not condone secret societies. Unofficially, they are all over the fucking place. The adult leaders who organize these clubs prefer to call them "honor societies," though when you look closely, there's little honor involved and much is hidden from public view. If the Boy Scouts survive this bankruptcy, I expect the end is nigh for these groups, if only for their blatant cultural appropriation of Native American traditions.

The US Scouting Service Project's website currently identifies 140 separate honor societies that have operated at Boy Scout camps since its founding, groups with names like something out of a story by H.P. Lovecraft: the Knights of Yawgoog, Clan of the Mystic Oak, the Black Diamond Society. The one almost every Scout knows about is the Order of the Arrow (OA) and, all things considered, it's the tamest of the bunch. It was founded in 1915 by E. Urner Goodman, who went on to become the national program director for the Boy Scouts of America, and Carroll A. Edison. Goodman was running a camp on Treasure Island on the Delaware River at the time. He wanted to create a fraternity that would encourage older Scouts to keep coming to camp. OA members have secret symbols and handshakes to identify participants, and much of its structure is inspired by Freemason rituals. The ceremony itself, which, of course, involves grown men dressed in loincloths and feather headdresses, contains elements of Lenni Lenape lore. Scouts are selected to participate based on how closely they adhere to the Scout Law. Once nominated, they must go through the Ordeal, which, when we did it at Camp Manatoc, in Ohio, meant the boy got one hard-boiled egg and one match and was sent into the woods to live alone for twenty-four hours, in contemplative silence. Over 1 million boys have completed the OA ordeal.

The oldest honor society is likely the Tribe of Gimogash, which operated out of camps around the Toledo, Ohio, area for decades. For the initiation ritual adult leaders would paint themselves in red face and dress in Native American garb, while candidates were bound together with rope and marched into a clearing surrounded by tee-pees. Each boy was then commanded to reach into three drums buried in the ground. One drum was filled with hot ashes, one with water, and one with dirt. The hot ash was a test of bravery, the water was to cleanse the body, and the dirt was to remind the boy that one day he, too, would die.

The Tribe of Ku-Ni-Eh was created in 1922 at a Boy Scout camp near Cincinnati. Candidates were awakened at midnight, blindfolded, and forced to hike until dawn. Then they took a bath in a tank of cold water. An arrow tattoo was then scraped into their arms with a needle.

The most popular secret society within Scouting, the Tribe of Mic-O-Say, still operates at camps in Missouri to this day. Harold Bartle was a two-time mayor of Kansas City, Missouri, in the mid-1950s and early 1960s, but before that, he was the executive director of the Cheyenne, Wyoming, Council of the Boy Scouts of America. During his tenure he created the Tribe of Mic-O-Say, based on Arapaho traditions. Bartle claimed to have been inducted into an Arapaho tribe, which gave him the name Chief Lone Bear, but this is likely no more than an apocryphal tale. Young Scouts are chosen to become members of the select tribe at a ceremony that takes place in front of the entire camp, where they must endure an atomic wedgie, according to one source. Underage boys wear nothing but loincloths and dance in front of everyone. At the end of the ordeal, Bartle himself would play "chief" and place an eagle's claw around the Scout's neck. Bartle, by the way, is also responsible for naming the local football team, the Kansas City Chiefs.

Today the Mic-O-Say program is a major draw for the Bartle

Scout Reservation summer camp. And like with Seven Ranges, the ties to its secret program have created a toxic, sexualized atmosphere among its staff members.

In 2017, after the Boy Scouts of America relaxed its policy on gender, allowing girls to formally join its ranks, a seventeen-year-old girl joined the staff at Bartle Scout Reservation for the summer. She lasted exactly twelve days. In a subsequent lawsuit filed against the camp for gender discrimination, sexual harassment, and a sexually hostile work environment, she alleged that the men on staff would speak about the size of their penises in front of her. One even carried around the book *How to Live with a Huge Penis,* which included a handy measuring tape. First-year staff members were assigned "older brothers," who took them into the woods and interviewed them about "sexually explicit" habits. She was made to change in a room without proper window coverings, and, on one occasion, an adult male walked in where she was naked and then left the door open for others to see inside.

"You would think that the Boy Scouts would have learned, based on all the lawsuits that have happened in recent years about child abuse," her attorney, Robin Koogler, told KCUR. "But now they're opening themselves up to do the same thing to young women."

Due to the lawsuit's resolution agreement, the victim can no longer speak publicly on the matter.

———————

According to the Troop 150 history website, the first Pipestone ceremony took place in the summer of 1926, at Camp Tuscazoar, which was the primary camp for Buckeye Council Scouts before the construction of Seven Ranges. The program was created by three prominent, local leaders: a Scout executive named George Deaver, a high school teacher named C.L. Riley, and I.W. Delp, the principal of Lehman High School, along with a boy named Charles Mills, a Scout skilled in theater production. Its stated purpose was to reward the service of the very best Scouts at Camp Tuscazoar. The Pipestone was a token to remind the boys of their time at camp and to serve as an incentive to return.

In 2023, the official website for Buckeye Council explains Pipe-stone in outdated, culturally tone-deaf terminology: *An Indian cere-mony was a natural choice of a vehicle to convey this message and token. The valley of Tascarawas was a prime area of Indian activity as attested by the history of the area.*

It goes on to warn: *The Pipestone Ceremony itself is not intended to be, or conducted as, an initiation or a hazing, and it is not to be represented to Scouts as such!*

If forcing kids to drink bitter liquid and sit between the legs of a nearly naked obese man is not an initiation, I don't know what you would call it.

The Pipestone token is unique to Seven Ranges. First-year grad-uates are given a simple square of red rock upon which is etched the pictograph of a stick-figure man holding a staff with both hands above his head. Each subsequent year the Scout must bring back his Pipe-stone and trade it in for a slightly longer one to signify how many years he has completed. An etching of a fire is added for second year, then a teepee, a flower, and, finally, an arrowhead. The red rock it's made of is catlinite, which is a type of soft claystone that has been pressed between layers of quartzite for millions of years. This par-ticular form of catlinite can only be found in one specific region of Minnesota, where it is mined by descendants of the Lakota people. It was named after George Catlin, an artist who traveled the American West and visited the Lakota quarries in 1835, capturing scenes of the Plains Indians in his paintings. The mineral is also known as "pipe-stone" because it's what the local tribes used to carve their pipes.

To better understand the history of Pipestone and the culture that has been exploited for the bizarre rituals at Seven Ranges, I traveled to Minnesota to speak to Travis Erickson, a man who still mines the rock.

Travis is a member of the Sisseton-Wahpeton Dakota Nation, a fourth-generation miner. He also serves as the spiritual advisor for the Keepers of Sacred Tradition of Pipemakers. His great-grandfather, Moses Crow, settled in Minnesota in 1927, and nothing about their

sacred process has changed since. Travis keeps a tidy storefront downtown, where visitors can stop in and buy one of his handmade pipes.
The quarry itself is just a mile down the road.

It was unseasonably warm when I visited in February after
catching a flight to Sioux Falls and driving in. Travis was at a carving
station inside and I pulled up a chair to sit beside him as he chiseled
an eagle's head out of the rock. His calloused hands were covered
in a fine red dust.

"I started young," he recalled. "My uncles brought me down to the
quarry when I was ten years old. I would break apart the quartzite and
throw it into rubble piles. I goofed off by carving smaller pieces of the
catlinite. When I was sixteen, they taught me how to carve a pipe."

Travis has five children of his own now and thirteen grandkids.
But none of them want to learn the old ways. He is probably the last
of his line.

His people tell many stories about how pipestone came to exist.
The most common legend is that there was once a great war between
tribes and the blood of the fallen leaked into the ground and painted
the stone red. They believe that the blood of their ancestors still
resides in the rock. But the story of the first ceremonial pipe and
where it came from is even more fantastic.

Nineteen generations ago, a great famine decimated the Lakota
people. Their chief sent his two best scouts to search for food beyond
their borders. On their walkabout one day, the scouts noticed a figure
in the distance, standing on a hill. It was a beautiful woman. Immediately one of the scouts was overcome with desire and ran after the
woman to have sex with her. But as he approached, a strange cloud
appeared and enveloped both the woman and the man. When it dissipated, the beautiful woman was still there, but all that remained of the
scout was his bones. This woman was called Ptesan Wi, and she was
part of the Wakan Tanka, the so-called Great Mystery, which encom-
passes everything sacred, divine, and unknowable. (I realize now that
the Walk-and-Talk Man of my memories was my eleven-year-old
brain misinterpreting this detail.) Ptesan Wi returned to the starving

tribe and gave to them the *chanunpa,* the sacred pipe, and taught them seven sacred ways to pray. She taught them to say their prayers into the pipe, into the tobacco, so that their requests could travel to the other realm as smoke. When she left, she promised to return one day. "When a white buffalo calf is born, it will be a sign that life's sacred loop will begin again," she said. But the story gets stranger if you know whom to ask.

Many years ago, an elder from Travis's tribe visited him as he carved a new *chanunpa.* "Do you know what the original pipe was made of? The one that Ptesan Wi gave to our chief?" the elder asked Travis.

"What was it?" I asked as he recounted the story.

"He told me it was made out of a gemstone from another world. He said it was brought here by the Star Nation People, from their home in the Pleiades star cluster."

"You believe it was brought here by . . . aliens?" I asked.

"We are the aliens," he said. "We come from out there. Not here. And we brought it with us."

Travis is a believer in many things, in the tenuous boundaries between this plane of reality and the dreamworld. When he was younger, Travis was tormented by a recurring dream of being chased by a bear. He came to believe that the bear was his spirit animal, his spiritual guide, and when he accepted that, the bear stopped chasing him. He honored the bear by getting its image tattooed on his body.

As he grew into his role as guardian of the quarry, the residents of Pipestone, Minnesota, came to consider Travis as their spiritual guide.

"People come to me with their dreams," he explained. "One day a woman came to see me because she kept having a dream about a horse. She'd had a horse years ago and it had passed away. I thought about her dream and I kept seeing this farmhouse in my mind. A farmhouse with a lone apple tree. When I told her this, she said that was the farm where her parents lived, where she had grown up. I told her to take an apple, cut it in half, and offer one half to the horse in her dreams. She did that and then she felt a great sense of relief and the horse never bothered her again."

The Pipestone ceremonies at Seven Ranges are a bastardization of Native American lore, especially that fourth-year speech about the dangers of homosexuality. In fact, the Lakota people readily accepted homosexuals within their tribe. They were the Winkte, and were believed to be of two spirits. When the chief would go off to war, he would leave his young daughters with the Winkte because he knew they would be safe with them.

"Homosexuality was natural," Travis said.

As our interview was winding down, I took out my Pipestone, the fifth-year stone I'd earned in 1995, shortly after Mike Klingler's death. I handed it to him. Or, I should say, I handed it back to him, because he was almost surely the man who first mined it out of the ground before executives from Buckeye Council purchased a block of catlinite from his store. He turned it around in his dusty fingers.

"I was hoping that you might carve something new on the back," I said.

I thought he would find the idea poetic, but when I suggested this, he looked uninterested. "What do you want me to carve?"

"I don't know."

He set it down on his table and continued to work on his eagle.

While I thought about what to have him carve, I walked around the store and perused the wares. I bought a pair of earrings for my daughter and some honey sticks for my son. Then I came around to a display of traditional pipes. Each pipe had a tag on it with the price and the name of the Native American who'd carved it. I found one that Travis had made and brought it to the counter.

"I got that design from Pete Muscle," he said. "He was this friend of mine who lived in town. After he died, I thought to make a pipe like his, but a pipe's design is specific to a person and you're not supposed to take someone else's. But I had a dream that night and in my dream I saw Pete Muscle. He was wearing a new shirt and he was laughing.

He was very content. He wanted me to know that it was okay. That I could make his pipe if I wanted to."

As he wrapped Pete Muscle's pipe, I had an inspired thought. I suddenly understood why I had brought my Pipestone all the way from Ohio back to its home.

"Instead of carving something on my Pipestone, would you bury it for me?" I asked.

Now Travis was interested. "Of course," he said. "It's what we do with our pipes. They hold a sort of magic, and when it's gone, we return the pipe to the ground. I can do that with your stone. But are you ready to let it go?"

I thought about it for a moment. "I am," I said.

then

On Sunday morning of Week Two, everything began again, with a fresh army of Scouts. Check-in, swim test, dinner, Retreat, Campfire. Summer at Seven Ranges is a lot like the movie *Groundhog Day*. There's a set routine and you live it again and again and again for eight weeks. I liked that very much. The routine refined us. We learned from our mistakes and each week we were a little better. I got better at teaching First Aid. I memorized the camp songs and gained confidence in my limited singing range. And friendships grew closer.

I began to notice that some of my friends who shared tents had pushed their beds together. If someone inquired, one might reply that they'd done so to open up the room to allow for more visitors during the day, and after everyone had gone, they separated the beds again for sleep. But that didn't explain the shared bedding that draped over both mattresses. There were two boys who lived by Waterfront that summer who acted quite like an old married couple, finishing each other's sentences, sharing inside jokes, never far from each other.

There was always enough doubt for deniability—they're just close friends, one might say. But on some level we knew, all of us. It just wasn't something that was ever addressed directly for fear of confirmation. I was jealous of such intimacy. How does one boy find another boy with similar interests? I wondered. The prospect seemed dangerous. Sometimes I thought about telling Trey how I adored him, telling him how his simple presence made me happy. But every such fantasy ended with imagined accusations and shame.

On Sunday morning of Week Two,

everything began again,

with a fresh army of Scouts.

Or worse, what if he laughed? I couldn't bear to spend the summer hiding in shame. It was best I simply stay quiet to preserve a real friendship.

That summer I took long walks across Seven Ranges whenever I could, for the purpose of getting lost in thought, trying to figure out myself, my real self, this self that was at odds with the traditions of where I was from and how I was raised. I favored the path that wound behind Handicraft to the chapel. It was soft underfoot, a carpet of pine needles. It smelled wonderful and the way the sunlight came through in pillared rays made it feel otherworldly. If you've ever been a camp counselor, perhaps you understand this feeling I've been trying to convey—the feeling that this was the real world, everything within the borders of Seven Ranges, and everything outside was miasma. In this world I felt safe to think these thoughts. Here's the cruel twist of life: When you find these safe places, they never last long.

I remember the last, innocent moment.

It was Week Three. A Tuesday. Another long day had ended and the sky was cloudless and I decided that I wanted to shower under the stars so that I could look up into the Big Dipper and the sweep of the Milky Way in the clothes God gave me. Seven Ranges is far from the light pollution of any major city, and the showers on the hill behind the dining hall have no roof and from there you can see for miles over the Ohio plains. It was late and nobody was there and I left off the lights so it would remain dark inside. I undressed and turned on a shower, staying away from the water until it got tepid. I stepped under the spray and then turned to look out at the world, and what I saw filled me with such profound wonder I've been chasing it ever since. All across the expanse were silent explosions of colorful lights, fireworks over the towns and farms of Central Ohio. They sparkled below a field of stars, mimicking their brilliance. I had forgotten it was the Fourth of July. I watched in awe for what seemed an hour until the fireworks died down and it was only the heavens above again. I felt favored by the universe. I don't think anybody else had seen the full spectacle that night. Not like I had.

Everything after that night is fractured in my mind.

Mike Klingler, not sane, held darkness within.

I felt it by then. It's easy to say that in hindsight. But I did. I felt it in the way he looked at me and some of the other boys at camp. I could feel the contemplation behind his eyes. It's an understanding that attractive boys share with women, I think. At some point you become aware that certain men desperately want to fuck you. It's in that look, a banal contemplation. They are imagining you naked and wondering how your skin feels to the touch, even when they're not saying it. Sometimes it's easy to ignore. Sometimes it's not. Depends on how well they can mask it. And that's not to say all men who have these thoughts are evil or insane. Quite the contrary—I think it's simply a natural instinct in our species. And I don't believe anyone is in control of their imagination. I believe we are the thing that is aware of our imagination. We are not our thoughts; we are our actions. The real question becomes, are we even in control of our actions? Let's hope we are. Otherwise, I don't know whom to blame.

Whenever I spoke to Mike Klingler, I had the distinct impression that he wanted me, but also that he had no desire to really know me. It was an odd feeling, to imagine yourself through someone else's eyes as nothing but a plaything.

Mike assaulted Tommy in his tent on Friday night when everyone was at Pipestone. I would learn the details many years later, when, working as a reporter, I got curious enough to pull the police reports.

Tommy was asleep in his tent when someone lifted the sidewall by his bed. Tommy was terrified, but stayed silent, trying not to wake his tentmate. The form moved closer and put a hand over Tommy's mouth. In the dim light he could see that it was Mike Klingler. Mike's breath reeked of alcohol.

Mike slid his other hand down Tommy's shorts, but Tommy

pulled away from Mike's grip. "Get out," he whispered. And Mike left as quietly as he'd appeared.

Tommy didn't tell anyone at first. The next day was Saturday. He went home and thought it over. On Sunday he came back to Seven Ranges, and when he went to bed that night, he set his pocketknife next to him on the bed in case Mike returned. His tentmate, Andrew Lund, spotted it and asked why he needed his knife. Tommy told him what had happened on Friday night, but left out the part where Mike put his hand down his pants.

On the following day, Monday, Tommy told Ben, the program director, about it. But he wouldn't say who it was and he left out the part where Mike had molested him. There was only so much Ben could do with that information. He had a talk with senior staff and told them they would be in serious trouble if they got caught bringing booze into camp.

Tommy asked to go home that night, but said he'd come back in the morning to teach the FROG group. He returned at 6:15 a.m.

I remember that day well. I took the Scouts in my First Aid class to the dining hall that morning. A nurse had come to camp to demonstrate CPR on a dummy, which we laid out on one of the dinner tables. The day was hot and muggy, cicadas hummed in the trees, a typical July day in rural Ohio. As the boys took turns performing mouth-to-mouth on the mannequin, I began to nod off. I was nearly asleep when I felt a hand on my ear, caressing me there. It felt so good to be touched and it was done in such a soft way, the way a girl might hold you before she kissed you. I pictured Becky as I turned around. But it was Mike. He didn't say anything. He just smiled and walked away.

That night Tommy led the FROG Scouts to Turkey Ridge for the weekly primitive-camping overnight excursion. Nine Scouts went on the trip, along with two adults.

The next morning I was checking knots by the door when Tommy walked by. I knew immediately that something terrible had happened. His skin was ashen gray and his ever-present smile was gone. His eyes were sunken and vacant. It was like there was nothing there but a body moving independently of consciousness. I felt its emptiness.

"Tommy," I said. "What happened?"

He shook his head and went inside. During breakfast I watched him from across the room. He put food on his plate, but didn't eat. He didn't talk to the Scouts around him. And when Norman tried to speak to him, he only shook his head again. Norman walked over to me.

"What the hell is going on?" I asked.

"Something bad," he said.

And then, just as the program was beginning, Tommy spotted Lucas. He got up and went to him. They spoke for a moment and then Lucas led him outside.

An hour later, I was in the First Aid station, prepping for class, when Lucas jogged in. He was manic and it took him a second to see me. "Renner," he said. "You have to pack up your stuff and put it in a tent in CIT-ville. Right away."

"What's going on?"

"I can't talk about it right now. Just please move your stuff out."

"Are you mad at me?"

Lucas sighed. "No. Something happened. Something is still happening. Some executives from counsel are coming down. Minors can't be found living in the dorms. I don't want you to get in trouble."

"Something happened to Tommy, didn't it?"

"James. Please."

"I understand. It's okay."

It took me five minutes to pack. By the time I was done, Lucas was gone again. I tucked my gear under a picnic table until class was over and then I walked it all down to CIT-ville and found my old tent, still empty. I walked over to Mike Klingler's tent beneath the pine canopy. It had been cleared out, everything except an old dresser.

I walked back to my tent and unrolled my sleeping bag over a thin blue mattress. I lay down and closed my eyes and considered my predicament. No hot water. No thermostat for the cold nights. Just a sparse canvas tent that smelled of mildew. But at least it was mine.

I dozed. How long I'm not sure. Eventually I was awakened by a rhythmic sound, the repetitive creaking of bedsprings. *Squeak, squeak, squeak.* Curious, I stepped lightly to the front flap of my tent and pulled it back a little. The sound was coming from the tent across from me and its flap was open just enough for me to see a young man, fully nude, lying on his bunk, masturbating. His prick tapered from a fine head to a thick circumference at the base. Suddenly the boy stopped midstroke. He stood and stepped out of his tent, checking both ways first, before walking to Mike Klingler's empty tent with his erect prick swinging in the breeze. I had to go round to the back of my tent to watch what he did next. The boy stepped inside Klingler's tent and stood over his bed, which was bare except for another blue foam mattress. He ejaculated onto the mattress and then wiped the rest off with his hand and flung it onto the canvas ceiling before returning to his tent, where he got dressed and walked away.

What the fuck is going on?

I got a lightheaded feeling then, like I'd been pulled halfway out of my body. I felt a sense of danger and I wondered again what could have happened to Tommy. It was obvious, now, that Mike Klingler was involved. I thought about how he'd touched my ear the day before. It was like he'd given up hiding his true self. I think I knew then what happened, even if I didn't know the specifics.

By lunch every staffer thought they had a piece of the story and we shared the news in whispers away from Scouts' ears. Some said that there had been a confrontation between Tommy and Mike up on Turkey Ridge. Some said Tommy made up a story about Mike bringing a beer to camp and that got him kicked out. The general mood was that we should be angry with Tommy for getting Mike in trouble. But whatever had happened up on Turkey Ridge, I doubted Tommy was at fault.

I was right, but I wouldn't learn the truth for many years. The Buckeye Council of the Boy Scouts of America did their best to keep it quiet.

always

Before I share the details of the horror that transpired at Seven Ranges in the summer of 1995, I would like to reflect on what I loved about the Boy Scouts and some of the experiences that made me want to become an Eagle Scout. Otherwise, you might not understand why I stayed.

When I was young, I craved adventure, to light out for the territories with my friends and go on epic quests that tested my courage and resolve. But my childhood was spent on a farm in rural Ohio, as far from any real adventure as one can get. And so I lived inside the stories of others. I read voraciously: Tolkien. C.S. Lewis. Poe. And, of course, Stephen King. I read *It* in the fourth grade, in between *The Great Brain,* by John Dennis Fitzgerald, and *Bunnicula,* by James Howe. On the weekends, when I ventured into the vast woods surrounding our property, I imagined that I was entering Narnia or Midworld and I would find myself on a journey to save the universe from some epic monster, and I would return later, nearly broken but triumphant, and find that no time had passed.

That's what drew me to the Boy Scouts—that craving for adventure. All I knew about Scouting was that our local troop went camping at least once a month. Joining the Scouts gave me a ticket to explore strange, new worlds with a gang of boys. We built shelters and carried knives and played at war and at night we gathered around the campfire and told ghost stories. I couldn't care less about merit badges and lessons on patriotism. Give me a backpack and a compass and set me free.

I signed myself up for Boy Scouts when I was ten. My stepmother

Photo by Linda Renner

Before I share the details of the horror

that transpired at Seven Ranges

in the summer of 1995,

I would like to reflect on what I loved

about the Boy Scouts

was against the idea, so when an assistant scoutmaster from Troop 558 passed out applications at school, I filled one out and turned it in without telling her. When that same assistant scoutmaster came to pick me up for my first meeting, she was too socially embarrassed to argue.

On my very first campout, I broke my wrist in a game of capture the flag, at a place called Twin Antlers, which was a primitive retreat in the wood line of a local farmer's field. For the Scouts of Troop 558, capture the flag was serious business. If you got caught by the other team, you were taken prisoner and held in a cell made of sticks, and your arms and legs were tied with twine so you couldn't escape. It was wonderfully dangerous. Anyway, I came down awkwardly on a big oak tree root while running from the other team and we all heard my wrist snap. Our scoutmaster, a rugged sheep rancher named Terry Porter, wrapped my arm in a magazine and drove me home. Later, at the hospital, the doctor complimented his makeshift splint and told me there were valuable lessons to be learned in Scouting if I paid attention.

At Camp Manatoc, where we visited each winter, the camp director would stop by our cabin at night and tell us the legend of Red Eyes. A hundred years ago, when Manatoc was first constructed, the camp ranger died in a terrible accident, he said—sometimes he drowned in the lake; sometimes he died when a tree fell on him. It varied depending on the teller. But they all agreed that the ranger was an exceptionally tall man, almost seven feet. This all happened during the Great Depression. Times were tough. Money was tight. And when the council leaders went to the undertaker, they discovered they did not have enough coin to purchase an oversized casket. So the camp staff bought a regular casket and decapitated the body so that it would fit inside. Forever after, the dead ranger has haunted Camp Manatoc and boys who sneak away from their troop might encounter the ranger's floating head on the path, his glowing red eyes searching the night for flesh.

I was tight with two older boys then—Toby and Jeremy. We

didn't care about Red Eyes. We liked to wait until everyone else was asleep and then tiptoe out of our tents and roam the campgrounds until 2 a.m., while Jeremy smoked cigarette butts he'd pilfered from ashtrays. One night, when I was about thirteen, I followed Toby and Jeremy outside and then down the dirt road that led away from Concord Lodge toward the old pool house. It was closed for the season, but the boiler room door was always unlocked and we liked to hang out inside and bullshit about music and girls. While on the way there, Toby noticed something in the woods, off the trail. He jumped, startled. I followed his gaze. There, in the dark, about fifty feet under the tree canopy, was a pair of red eyes staring back at us.

"Holy shit," said Jeremy.

"What the fuck is that?" said Toby.

To this day I don't know what came over me. I think I wanted to show the older boys that I was brave, that I wasn't frightened of anything. Because what I did next was let out an Indian war cry and run into the woods, directly toward the glowing eyes. And when I came to it, I discovered the two demon eyes were really indicator lights on an oil derrick hidden in the trees. Of course, my friends didn't know this and so I screamed like I was being murdered and they took off toward camp faster than I'd ever seen them run.

I discovered a love for theater by way of performing in Campfire skits. Sometimes Toby would play a character named Mr. Herman, where he would prop himself up on the ledge of a cabin's kitchen pass-through with a poncho over his shoulders, his hands in a pair of shoes. I'd pass my arms through the poncho on either side so that it looked like he was a little person. Then Toby would go about his morning routine of washing his face and brushing his teeth, except I couldn't see anything and he had no control over his "arms" and it got ridiculously messy. There was another skit that Toby and I became known for, which was unceremoniously banned from ever being performed again at Camp Manatoc. The scene opens with a glass of water and a toothbrush resting on a stool. A boy passes by eating some cookies, spots the items, and takes the opportunity to brush his teeth like a good Scout, spitting all the crumbs back into the glass. A second Scout, this one eating a slice of pizza, passes by and does the same thing. A third Scout, gnawing at a chicken wing, comes by then, brushes his teeth and spits into the glass. By now, the water inside has turned into a milky mess. That's when I come in. I say, "Oh, look, a glass of milk!" And then I chug the entire thing. We did that skit only twice and then someone puked and we couldn't do it anymore.

More than anything, I loved being on the water. In canoes, tubes, sailboats, whatever. During our weeks at Seven Ranges, we would swamp canoes by the shore, our heads inside the upside-down vessel, pretending we were in a submarine. Once, on a ten-mile canoe trip down the Mohican River, me and a couple other boys were caught in a downpour and rapids formed around us, making the journey quite treacherous. A friend of mine, Jason, came around a bend and encountered a fallen oak tree. The churning waters sucked him right down. One moment he was there; one moment he was gone. We waited a few seconds, but he didn't come up. He was stuck inside the canoe and the canoe was holding him underwater. I raced over and brought my boat up parallel to the tree so that when it caught, it held tight against the trunk. I reached down and found his head about six inches below. I grabbed hold of his chin and wrenched him out from the canoe and he popped out and drifted downstream, where he was able to climb onto the bank. I'm pretty sure he would have drowned after another ten seconds or so. The Chinese have a saying: Once you've saved a man's life, you're responsible for it forever. But I have no idea what became of him. Hopefully, he treated people well.

Every February, our troop went on a Klondike camp, which is where you set up tents on the snow and survive the weekend the best you can in the Ohio weather. During one winter the staff at Manatoc had a Klondike contest to see which troop was best at orientation and set clues around camp that gave coordinates to locations around the property, where you would find more coordinates

More than anything,

I loved being on the water.

to take you farther, and then on and on until you found a stuffed groundhog, which was the prize. I was good with the compass and I led a few of our Scouts around camp that day. I remember how quiet it was, every sound muffled by snow, the thick flakes falling all around us. We marched around, hunting the groundhog, our feet dry and snug in our boots, our pants duct-taped around them to keep out the moisture. And we found that groundhog before anyone else that year. Our only prize, the honor of it all.

In the spring we usually visited Camp Beaumont on the Pennsylvania border and stayed in a cabin with a large, shared room full of bunk beds. At night that room got steamy hot from the fire in the fireplace, the air thick with the smell of sweaty young men. At lights-out the scoutmaster would play a cassette tape of Stephen King's *The Mist,* narrated by the actor William Sadler, whom I would meet on a movie set in LA ten years later while I was working as a production assistant.

It was at Beaumont that a friend introduced me to a new card game, *Magic: The Gathering,* and it consumed our lives for a couple years. We saved our money to buy new card packs and traded minions and lands on campouts, in between battles.

I think there's something about the Boy Scouts that appeals to young men who do not enjoy playing sports or participating in afterschool clubs. Our meetings and campouts followed an unwavering routine. There was a military-like structure to it. Meetings began with a flag ceremony and a roster call. Then we divided into patrols, where we discussed the upcoming business of meal prep for excursions. There was merit badge time; an organized game; then the closing ceremony, where we gathered in a circle and crossed our arms and held hands with the Scouts on either side of us while we said a prayer. There was no routine at home—I never knew what to expect—but in Scouting everything was predictable. It was the place without anxiety. Until it wasn't.

I rose in rank through the years, from Scout to patrol leader, to senior patrol leader. I planned campouts, carried out the old

I grew up on a farm in the country

before the Internet, so I already knew

how to swim like a fish.

routines. I don't know if I can go so far as to say that Scouting saved my life, but it did make it manageable.

After Klingler died, I stayed because the routine of camp provided the only semblance of order. And because that's where my friends were.

now

I've read through the police reports several times and every time I do, it makes me ill. You can skip this chapter if you want, I don't mind. If you do, go forward knowing that Tommy survived a terrible assault by the skin of his teeth. However, I've come to believe that it's the *not wanting to know* that blinded the Boy Scouts of America for so long. Knowing the dark details makes it harder to continue a program that allows for such things to happen again and again. So I strongly suggest you stay.

The following narrative is taken from the investigative reports of the Beach City Police Department and the Stark County coroner, as well as a detailed statement written by Lucas Taylor.

About 11 p.m. on July 12, two staff members hiked up to Turkey Ridge, on the outskirts of Seven Ranges, to visit Tommy and his group of young Scouts who were spending the night in some old Adirondacks, which are wide, wooden platforms with three walls and a roof for shelter. The boys went to sleep and then Tommy went to bed, too. Before the two older staff members left, they woke up Tommy to let him know they were heading back to the main camp, leaving him alone with the boys and a scoutmaster, who'd come along as a chaperone. Eventually Tommy fell back asleep. Sometime later, he was shaken awake by Mike Klingler. He didn't know what time it was. Mike pulled Tommy's blanket off him and asked him to come out of the Adirondack. As Tommy was getting up, the scoutmaster stirred and asked if anything was wrong.

"It's okay," Tommy told him.

Outside, Mike asked Tommy if each of the nine FROG Scouts were accounted for. "I only count eight," he said.

When Tommy turned to count the sleeping bodies, Mike grabbed him by the back of the shirt and dragged Tommy away from the group to an empty Adirondack on the other side of Turkey Ridge.

"What's wrong?" Tommy asked. "What did I do?"

But Mike would not answer him.

"Mike, I didn't do anything. I didn't say anything."

"Bullshit," said Mike. "You were spreading rumors. You told people I was drinking at camp." He punched Tommy. The boy fell to the ground. Mike kicked him hard. He knelt down and put his hands around Tommy's throat and squeezed. Tommy couldn't breathe.

After a moment Mike relaxed his grip and pulled Tommy behind the Adirondack. Out of sight Mike undressed. Then he forced Tommy to touch his erect penis. Afraid, Tommy complied. When he was done, Mike smeared the ejaculate on Tommy's face.

"You're fucking gay," Mike told him. He pulled Tommy over to a tree. "Put your arms around the trunk," he commanded. When Tommy hugged the tree, Mike pulled Tommy's pants down. "There's poison ivy on the tree, so you better not move much. If you tell anyone about any of this, I'll kill you. Understand?"

"Yes."

Finally he sent Tommy back to his group. Mike disappeared into the night. Tommy sat in the dark for hours. He didn't go back to sleep. He didn't tell the adult chaperone. He didn't want to ruin the boys' overnight campout. When the sun came up, Tommy led the Scouts back to the main camp. Then he took a shower and went to the dining hall.

Around 7:25 a.m., while at breakfast, Tommy spotted Lucas and asked him if he had any free time that day to talk. Lucas, God bless him, said he was free right now. Lucas took Tommy downstairs to the boiler room, the only place with complete privacy. Tommy started talking. At first, he once again omitted the molestation. He showed Lucas the injuries he got the night before: a bruise on the inner-right thigh, three abrasions on his lower back, various bruises on his pecs and abdomen. Tommy also said he had ringing in his inner right ear and soreness around his neck from being choked. At this point he still hadn't revealed the name of the man who assaulted him. He didn't know whom he could trust. Camp staff can be a tight fraternity. And also there was the first lesson of Pipestone that we'd all learned as children: A brave never tells.

Lucas told Tommy to wait in the boiler room for his safety, to avoid any interactions until the perpetrator was known. He told Tommy that he needed to share this information with Scooter. Lucas found the camp director upstairs and told him he needed to hear what Tommy was saying. So Tommy was brought upstairs to Scooter's room. Scooter asked Tommy directly who hurt him.

"Mike Klingler," Tommy said.

"Start from the beginning," Scooter said. This time Lucas took notes.

Lucas interviewed Tommy for two hours. The boy finally opened up about everything. This wasn't a fight. This wasn't bullying. This was rape. This was the threat of murder. This was beyond anything that could be contained or managed. When Scooter returned, Lucas briefed him on the new details. Then Scooter called Jack Johnson, the Scout executive for Buckeye Council. When the call was over, he started drafting an official letter for Mike's dismissal.

Johnson sent Don Schneck, program director for the entire Buckeye Council, down to Seven Ranges to personally escort Klingler off the premises. But first, Schneck walked Mike to his tent and stood nearby as he packed his things. Mike appeared to be very agitated. As he gathered his clothes, Mike mumbled to himself. Schneck listened, catching words here and there. "I had a lot of responsibility that summer," Mike said. "Then there was the fire . . . It was a lot of responsibility."

He kept talking about the fire, but what he was saying wasn't making any sense.

"What about my paycheck?" he asked Schneck. Before the man

could answer, he said, "Never mind. My insurance will take care of everything."

Schneck didn't know what he meant by insurance. Insurance for what? Schneck walked Mike to the parking lot and watched him drive away.

Mike returned to Beach City, where he lived with his parents. He told his mother he'd been in a fight at camp and had to leave. He lay down and took a nap.

Ten-year-old Nicole Weisgarber, who lived next door, went outside to jump on the trampoline behind her home. Her mother, Janette, was on the phone in the kitchen, keeping an eye on her girl. They both saw Mike walk into the field out back carrying a rifle. He liked to shoot groundhogs back there, so they didn't think much of it.

Then a shot rang out and Janette looked outside in time to see Mike's legs fly up into the air. Realizing something was wrong, she and Nicole ran out to check on him. They walked to the fence and from there they could see Mike's body on the ground.

"I think he's hurt," Janette said.

"I do, too," said Nicole.

"Go get Mary Ann."

Nicole ran to the Klingler house to get Mary Ann, Mike's mother. Janette, meanwhile, ran back inside and called 911.

The ambulance got there before the police. The EMTs began to administer CPR the way I taught it at camp—fifteen compressions, two breaths. Then the police arrived. They noted Mike's rifle, a Winchester .22, was leaning against a tree. Mary Ann told them that she had picked it up and placed it there after finding her son. They checked it over. There was one round chambered, three in the magazine. The EMTs continued CPR as they loaded Mike onto a backboard and then into the ambulance.

The police interviewed Mary Ann before they left. They asked her if Mike was depressed, if he was upset about anything. She told them that he had been at Scout camp all week and had come home early because of an "incident." But she did not elaborate.

Mike was pronounced dead upon arrival at the hospital.

The Stark County coroner inspected the body and listed cause of death as "undetermined," though he suggested it was likely an accident. *It appears as though the decedent slipped and fell on the rocky terrain where he was shooting, causing the gun to fire,* he wrote. *The parents deny threats of suicide or depression.*

There were no drugs or alcohol found in his system.

Years later, while working as a reporter, I spoke with Richard Walters, who investigated Mike's death for the Stark County coroner. It was no accident, he said, contrary to how the report is written. "We couldn't prove if he did it or somebody else did it," he told me. "There was evidence that he had been involved in an altercation with someone at camp. Because of that, it's possible somebody else could have been involved. And that's why the case was listed as undetermined. We were unable to prove it was a suicide or a homicide."

The way the bullet had gone into his body meant that Mike might have leaned on the rifle and pulled the trigger with his toes, or someone had placed the barrel against his chest and fired. "I'm being the devil's advocate," said Walters. "But this is the kind of business we're in. We're in the devil's advocate business."

then

My memories of the days surrounding Mike Klingler's death are fractured and incomplete.

I remember the next morning best, how the staff was called to the picnic tables behind the dining hall after breakfast. Lauren wasn't there. She'd gone to Ecology already, and I thought we really should wait until someone called her back, but we didn't. I remember Scooter's face and how he looked like he'd aged ten years overnight. All of a sudden he looked like a real adult.

"I want you to hear it from me first," he said. "Yesterday I fired Mike Klingler. He went home, got his gun out, and shot himself. He committed suicide."

My ears started ringing. I looked around at my friends. Norman stared at the ground. Trey looked at me, wide-eyed. I'd never known someone who'd committed suicide. In fact, I'd never known anyone who had died. That might sound strange. I was seventeen years old, after all, but it's true. It's one benefit to having very young parents—all my grandparents were still around.

"Why was he fired?" someone asked.

I don't remember what Scooter said, or if he even answered the question. I don't remember anything between that moment and an hour later, when we were all called back again. This time Scooter was frantic. "I've been told the coroner made a mistake," he said. "Apparently, Mike was shooting at pop cans in his backyard and a bullet ricocheted off a tree and hit him in the chest."

"But . . . why did they think it was suicide?" someone asked.

But Scooter couldn't say. It struck me that he didn't know much

My memories of the days
surrounding Mike Klingler's death
are fractured and incomplete.

more than we did and he was trying to hang on to an image of stead-fast authority for our benefit and it was taking a great toll on him. In a couple days Scooter would leave camp with a terrible case of shingles, brought on by the stress of it all.

I don't remember how that week ended. I don't remember anything more until the tornado.

now

There is a magic elixir that tastes good, and when you drink it, it makes you happy. It gives you confidence. It gets rid of all the bad memories and fills your heart with love. And it's cheap: $10 can get you loaded if you shop the state stores and you're not picky. What a miracle! Why wouldn't you drink it every day, as much as you can, always and forever? Because, and here's the Faustian twist, this elixir is also poisonous. Drink too much, you die. Drink almost too much, you die slowly. Fuck me, right? And it can always be found nearby, this dangerous solution to sadness. I've got three liquor stores within a five-minute drive. I prefer to visit the scary one, downtown, where the guy slides your liquor under the glass. The cashiers don't make eye contact. Nobody judges you downtown.

Vodka is my poison of choice. Midshelf. Smirnoff. Red label. I don't savor it. I drink it to get drunk. I mix it with lime soda water to keep the calorie count down. My family can't tell how much vodka is in it if I mix it with soda water. I don't measure by shot. I pour until we're halfway. From March 13, 2020, the day COVID began for real in the States, until I lost my mind on April 12, 2022, I drank every single day. I'd buy a handle of red-label Smirnoff every few days from the Acme state liquor market, because that's the closest one to me. Most times I'd add a bottle of Jameson, too. I started drinking around 3 p.m., and I would smoke some pot at 7 p.m. I use those one-hitters that look like cigarettes. I'd pack it twice. Then an hour later, I'd pack it twice more. Does that even sound bad? It's not rock star bad, certainly. It's not Hunter. S. Thompson, Chivas and cocaine all night bad. It's rather embarrassing in contrast. Seriously, what a middle-aged, middle-class, white-guy habit. Of course, I also took Oxy when I could get it. Nobody else in my family likes narcotics. I don't understand that. What's not to like? When Casey, my teenage son, got a bottle after having his wisdom teeth removed and it was still sitting in the cabinet a month later, I claimed it, pill by pill. Why should they go to waste? And if you've never had the pleasure, oh! Oxy wraps your soul in a warm blanket of confident safety like the way your mum tucked you in at night when you were two. You feel good, man. You take the pill and you feel good. Why wouldn't you take it? Because, if you take, like, five, in quick succession, it gets its hooks in you and demands sacrifice. And eventually a lovely voice will whisper to you, *Psst, you know, heroin is easier to find. And a dealer never asks for proof of pain.*

I quit everything after my breakdown. My sobriety lasted six weeks. Then I went on vacation with my wife's extended family. Nothing too special, a house on Lake Erie for a week, where the algae blooms and the water isn't so good for swimming. Julie's family drinks. Good people, but professional drinkers. They bring a fully stocked liquor cabinet on vacation, complete with Aperol and vermouth. They enjoy making obscure mixed drinks from decades-old cocktail books. I'm not going to be the guy sipping La Croix in the background as everyone else shares a pitcher of Manhattans. So I drank.

The main argument against steady drinking is that it's unhealthy—that if you stop drinking so much, you will prolong your life. Stop drinking and die at ninety instead of sixty-five. But I've never seen that as much of an incentive. This world is full of teeth. The Buddhist understand that life is suffering. Longevity is a shit excuse for sobriety.

Ah, but that's the booze talking. Tricky, ain't it?

Alcohol is a depressant. It's very easy to forget this simple fact, because it also brings euphoria. That euphoria is the explosion created when all your serotonin flames out in a grand finale of the soul. You feel like shit the next day because all your happy chemicals are gone and all that remains is char. Maybe you're like me and your body has forgotten how to make serotonin by itself because you've provided it in the form of drugs for so long. I rely on medications like Citalopram to help me regulate my serotonin now. And if I just leave it alone, if I let the meds do their job, I'll feel better soon. Objectively, I know this. I know that if I just don't drink for ten days, if I can fight that urge, then the world starts to look good again. If I can reach that event horizon, I no longer crave alcohol because I no longer need it to have some optimism about this absurd dumpster fire of a world, where the atmosphere is filling up with CO_2 and my job is inviting myself into the tragedies of others. But life doesn't wait patiently for ten days, does it? Life gets in the way and it's really fucking hard to hold out, when you can feel happy right now even for just a little bit.

I have a podcast, *True Crime ThisWeek*. Every Friday morning I recap all the big stories in true crime. I devote my entire Thursday to it. I comb through Drudge Report and CNN and, yes, even Fox, culling stories of murder and mayhem. I pick only the cases that interest me and I avoid the real downers, like family annihilators and dead babies found in rest stop bathrooms. But I have to see those headlines when I dive deep. And it's easier to do it if I'm buzzed. So I made a deal with myself that I could drink on Thursdays—but only Thursdays! That way I could stay happy while reading all that junk.

Instead of bringing home a handle, on Thursdays I would buy a pint. That way I wouldn't leave anything in the cupboard to tempt me the next day. This went on for a couple weeks before Julie caught on to my new routine.

"How many was that?" she asked one Thursday evening when I poured myself a vodka and Diet Coke.

"Just one," I said.

"One what? One drink?'

"One pint."

"What?"

"One pint."

"You drank an entire pint?"

"I did, yes. It's just to take the edge off."

"Do you know how many shots that is? It's like eight to ten. If I had eight shots, I would be obliterated. You don't even seem drunk."

"I'm not drunk."

I think that's when she realized I had a real problem.

When it comes to drinking, my mind refuses to do the math. One pint sounds a lot better than ten shots. Julie's discovery was enough to wake me up a bit; to see that, yes, there was a problem. Yes, undeniably. I stopped drinking again. But not for long. There's always an excuse to start again: meeting up with an old friend at a corner bar, getting through small talk at a wedding reception. There are all sorts of potholes along the road to bump you off the wagon. And I steer toward them.

I have an old friend, Eddie, who lives down the street. He likes to meet at this whiskey bar called South Point Tavern. It's tucked inside the strip mall behind the pet rescue. The bartender puts out cups of Gardetto's if you tip her. The deeper I got into this book, the more I began to think about Eddie.

Eddie Rambler was an MP for the Marine Corps in Quantico. After a night of drinking off base, he pulled to the side of the highway to sleep off his buzz. A cop found him, woke him up. He avoided a DUI, but was charged with disorderly conduct and taken to jail. His superior came to collect him. They conducted a search of his apartment and discovered that he had more beer than the allotted six that were allowed for personal consumption. The misdemeanor itself wasn't such a big deal, but the repercussions for Eddie within the corps were. He was ridiculed and harassed for his fuckup. He lost his gig as an MP and was transferred to the armory. When the bullying became too overwhelming, he sought mental help and his guns were taken away. He managed to get honorably discharged after two years, but it wasn't easy. Eddie didn't contract PTSD from a war zone. No, he got it from the constant attacks by his peers on American soil. He's on 70 percent disability now, and as long as I've known him, he's been fighting with the Department of Veterans Affairs to get on full. His overwhelming anxiety prohibits him from holding down a regular job. He survives on government assistance and supplements his meager pay by cruising the neighborhood on trash pickup nights to see if there's a gizmo he can salvage and resell. He's very good at rehabbing dirt bikes and electric scooters.

Eddie has joint custody of a ten-year-old girl named Sarah. She's my daughter's age. And maybe Eddie can't hold down a job, but he does right by his girl. She's fed and clothed and happy. She has a tiny hamster named Marvin. When Eddie's car shit the bed last year, I started picking up Sarah on the way to school in the mornings. She rides in the back with my daughter, Laine, and they talk memes. I keep breakfast bars in the console for Sarah, but she never accepts them. Some days she jumps in with a bag of Flamin' Hot Cheetos or leftover pizza.

I found myself thinking about Eddie more and more while researching this book because like the US Marines who've developed PTSD and are now searching for help, there are eighty-two thousand former Boy Scouts who have suffered trauma. Meanwhile, nobody seems to be thinking about how to treat the long-term psychological issues that come from such abuse, stuff you can't fix with settlement money. How do you heal eighty-two thousand men? And who should foot the bill?

There have been some interesting advancements in the treatment of veterans suffering from PTSD in the last few years. One organization has conducted experiments that show it might be relatively easy and cheap to cure PTSD with the use of the drug Ecstasy and other psychedelics. Not treat it. *Cure it.* The organization is called MAPS, which stands for Multidisciplinary Association for Psychedelic Studies.

MAPS was founded in 1986 by Rick Doblin, PhD, a psychotherapist who personally witnessed the therapeutic benefits of Ecstasy before it was labeled a Schedule I substance, placing it into the same category as heroin. Before it became illegal in 1985, Dr. Doblin treated a young woman who suffered from PTSD after a sexual assault. He gave her Ecstasy in a controlled, therapeutic setting. The unique properties of the drug allowed his patient to become aware of the loops of negative thoughts that were contributing to her suicidal urges, to finally recognize her thoughts objectively, and to separate herself from them. Not only did she not commit suicide, she went on to become a therapist herself and is still alive today. So, how was something so beneficial ever placed into the same category as heroin?

Ecstasy is the street name for 3,4-methylenedioxymethamphetamine, referred to in the scientific community as MDMA. If it's in crystal form and not a tablet, it's called Molly, which has become the drug of choice at raves because it makes you feel euphoric and lasts for several hours. MDMA loads up your mind with serotonin, that happy chemical. It has limited psychedelic effects as well. It was first developed by a Merck chemist in 1912, but nobody recognized how fun it could be until the US Army commissioned a study on psychedelics in the 1950s at the University of Michigan, in Ann Arbor. That study found its way to the chemist Alexander Shulgin, who liked it so much he started recommending it to psychotherapists in the 1970s. Shulgin called the drug "window," because it seemed to open up his mind like a window, to allow him to perceive the world more clearly. Sometimes he called it his "low-calorie martini." Other therapists called the drug "Adam," because some believe that it returned users to a state of primordial innocence.

But just as MDMA was beginning to show promising results, President Reagan ruined everything. He and Nancy were promoting the whole "Just Say No" campaign and waging a war on all street drugs. To support their position, the conservatives only had to show pictures of the debauchery that was happening nightly at dance clubs like Studio 54, where Ecstasy was passed around like candy. Is this what we want America to look like? Can we go back and just say yes? On May 31, 1985, the DEA announced an emergency Schedule I classification for the drug.

Since then, Rick Doblin and his team at MAPS have patiently lobbied Congress to chill out and bring back Molly and her psychedelic sisters. Finally, in 2004, they were given permission to conduct clinical trials to study the effects of MDMA-assisted therapy on PTSD.

The timing made sense, since the first soldiers to see action in the War on Terror were returning home, bringing with them the effects of untold trauma.

"People who have PTSD have brains that are different from those of us who don't have PTSD," Doblin explained in a 2019 TED Talk, which has been viewed over 22 million times. "They have a hyperactive amygdala, where we process fear. They have reduced activity in the prefrontal cortex, where we think logically. And they have reduced activity in the hippocampus, where we store long-term memory."

But here's the magic of Ecstasy: MDMA reduces activity in the amygdala, increases activity in front cortex, and allows a traumatic memory to move into long-term storage, where it's no longer at the front of our every waking thought. It is practically designed to treat PTSD.

Doblin's initial study included 107 subjects. One was a veteran on disability due to PTSD, whom he refers to as "Tony." Like his other subjects, Tony participated in a therapeutic routine that included three sessions under the influence of MDMA separated by four sessions of traditional therapy. While taking the drug, Tony would lie on a couch and listen to music while experiencing the effects of MDMA. Whenever he wanted, he could speak to two therapists stationed on either side of his bed. During one session Tony had an epiphany. He realized that his PTSD was how his mind was trying to keep him connected to his friends who had died overseas. It was a way of honoring them. He was able to shift his perspective, to see himself in the eyes of his dead friends, to realize that they would not want him to suffer. There was a better way to honor their memory—to live his life as fully as possible. He has remained free of the symptoms of PTSD ever since.

After this study MAPS presented its findings to the FDA. They had cured 23 percent of patients suffering from PTSD using traditional therapy only. When they combined therapy with monitored use of MDMA, they were able to cure 56 percent. Ecstasy more than doubled their success rate. And when they checked in with their subjects a year later, another 10 percent reported that they also had no further symptoms. Two-thirds of their subjects had been healed.

The FDA described the MDMA technique as a "breakthrough therapy." Because of the MAPS success, the government was finally willing to reconsider psychedelics. They loosened restrictions on MDMA for study, and not just MDMA. They opened the door for psilocybin as well. Derived from magic mushrooms, psilocybin is a natural psychedelic, the favorite medicine of tripping hippies who want to see the face of God.

Doblin predicts that there will soon be thousands of clinics across the United States where therapists can administer MDMA and psilocybin to treat psychological disorders or to use the substances to promote empathy during couples counseling. "The psychedelic renaissance is here," he promised.

Since his TED talk, the cities of Denver, Oakland, and Ann Arbor have decriminalized psilocybin.

And that is of particular interest to me, because the other thing that psilocybin is very good at treating is alcoholism. Bill Wilson, the cofounder of Alcoholics Anonymous, thought of psychedelics as the secret Thirteenth Step for recovering addicts, according to the author Don Lattin. Step Two of AA states that we "came to believe that a Power greater than ourselves could restore us to sanity." But there are some stubborn alcoholics who cannot feel that higher awareness. Tripping balls will make you feel that higher awareness. Lattin discovered old letters between Wilson and Father Ed Dowling, a Catholic priest, in which he talked about taking psychedelics: *I am certain that LSD experiment has helped me very much. I find myself with a heightened color perception and an appreciation of beauty almost destroyed by my years of depressions.*

Wilson was considering making LSD an actual component of the program, but it was too controversial to do so at the time. It's interesting to consider the possibility that AA might not yet be complete.

"I've been reading about psilocybin," I told Eddie Rambler one

Tuesday night at South Point. Eddie enjoys ciders. When we're there, I drink Bulleit Rye.

"Psilocybin?"

"Magic mushrooms."

"Go on."

"There's this group out of Washington, doing studies on soldiers with PTSD," I told him. "They put veterans into a controlled environment, with therapists in the room with them, and then they give them psychedelics."

"Oh yeah? I mean, I'd try anything. Mushrooms have to be better than meth."

I had a lead on some mushrooms. But before I connected Eddie, I wanted to be sure it was real.

Trey returned to Ohio for the holidays in 2022. We met at Larry's bar, on Market. I was pretending not to drink that day, so I got a soda. My plan was to confess to him that I'd had a crush on him when we were kids. I wanted to say it out loud and not be ashamed of it anymore. I wanted him to hear it from me before he read it in this book.

He really does look like a young David Caruso now. He's grown more serious with age, quieter, but sometimes that old puckish grin escapes. I was not surprised to discover that Trey has a similar relationship with alcohol as I do, though for different reasons.

"I can have one drink, but if I have two drinks, I'll have ten," he explained to me. He doesn't consider it an addiction, though. It's a form of self-medication. His mind is too busy and it's the best way he's found to quiet it down. He suspects he has ADHD but doesn't know for sure.

"Can I tell you something?" he said. "I really hate the name Trey. That was a nickname my family gave me. My name's Wyatt."

We talked for over an hour and he helped me remember a great many things about the summer of 1995. It took about ten minutes to fall back into our old conversational cadence. I think if you go through some shit with someone—be it the military, the Boy Scouts, whatever—those shared life experiences sync up your personalities, like entangled photons that hold similar spins no matter how far apart they travel. His memory of the days around Mike's death were similarly jumbled and the rest of the summer was not as clear in his mind. If I had to guess, I'd say all of us suffered from memory loss caused by the shock of it all.

It's impossible not to talk about Mike Klingler without also talking about a man named Jim Mills, whom we met later that summer. The two are always connected, the dark matter equivalent of our entwined photons of light. I realized he might not have heard how his story ended.

"Did you hear about Jim Mills?" I asked.

"No."

"He committed suicide," I told him. "Shot himself the day his trial was supposed to start."

"No shit?"

There's no room in a conversation like this to say, "You know, I was kind of in love with you when we were kids." At our age, after all of this, maybe such revelations are simply untenable.

So I told him, instead, about my plan to explore psilocybin as a means to overcome my addictions.

"Do it," said Trey—I can't manage to call him Wyatt yet. "I've taken shrooms on a few occasions. If you ever get a chance, do it outdoors. There's something about feeling the grass on your feet and having the stars over your head, it's like you become a part of nature again."

"Any other advice?" I asked.

"Yes," he said, his eyes suddenly cold. "If you see anything that resembles your ego in there, kill it."

then

The storm came out of the west, boiling black clouds like the Nothing.

The day was hot and the only relief was the shade inside my tent down in CIT-ville. I had just finished my shift at the Trading Post and I was lazing on my bunk, thinking dark thoughts. I knew the story we'd been told about Mike Klingler was bullshit. Whatever happened between him and Tommy had been more than a fight. Mike was dead. And Tommy had not returned. He left a six-pack of IBC root beer behind. Nobody wanted to drink it.

I was in that realm between waking and dreaming, when I heard someone shouting from the scoutmaster's patio by the dining hall. I could tell by the tone of the man's voice that something else had gone wrong. I bounced out of bed and ran up the hill. I didn't recognize it at the time, but this was a fundamental shift in my behavior, the pivot between childhood and adulthood, I suppose. Before that day I ran away from danger. After Mike Klingler, however, I ran toward it. But please don't confuse it with some sense of being heroic. I think maybe the people that run toward danger are seeking a high, like any other addict.

There were three older staff members huddled together under the tarp roof by the soda machines, where the scoutmasters gathered before meals. The Ecology director, a young man named Ian Shore, who had the most magnificent blond Afro, was making excited hand gestures and glancing at the sky as he argued with the other two.

"We should fire the cannon," one of the men said. Firing the cannons was a big deal at Seven Ranges. Three bursts from the cannon

The storm came out of the west,

boiling black clouds like the Nothing.

was the emergency all-call, a notice to every troop to send their senior patrol leaders to the dining hall to gather further instructions.

"There's no time for all that back and forth," Ian said. "Let's just run out to the camps and send everyone in."

"What's happening?" I asked.

"There's a tornado on the ground outside Canton," Ian said. "I was on the phone with my mother when it touched down. She's in the basement now. It's coming our way."

Above us, the sky was blue and the sun shone down and everything was fine. But to the west, above the treetops, I saw a wall of night, an inky-black wall of angry clouds, and in the distance, just above the level of perception, I heard the first rumbles of thunder. I had never seen anything like it. Total blackness, like a void. I thought of a novella I'd read by Stephen King, *The Langoliers*. It's about this group of people on a plane who land in a deserted world that has shifted out of time. That world is being devoured by monsters munching their way toward the airport from the horizon, turning everything behind them into blank space. At that moment it seemed as if the Langoliers were on their way. It sure sounded like it.

"Do you want me to go, too?" I asked.

"No," said Ian. "Stay here and help the Scouts that come to the dining hall. Close all the windows. Keep everybody away from the glass."

And with that, Ian ran away, up the hill toward Mingo Mesa, and the other two staffers ran in opposite directions. I went inside the dining hall and helped close the windows overlooking the lake. Ben, the program director, arrived. He had a walkie-talkie on his hip, which connected him with Scooter at Admin.

"Tornado warnings for Stark and Columbiana Counties," I could hear Scooter say.

"Copy that," said Ben.

I watched the world grow dark outside. It happened fast, the way a total solar eclipse does, so quickly that it plays with your senses. Your mind protests at the unexpected night. A line of shadow swept across Lake Donahey and with it came a cool breeze. The temperature dropped precipitously. My arms broke out in gooseflesh.

The first Scouts came down the trail from behind the dining hall, where Ian had gone, the boys shouting, excited at the change in routine. A sudden, loud thunderclap silenced them.

I opened the door and they scrambled inside. "Take a seat at a table near the back," I said. "Don't worry if it's not where your troop usually sits. No, that's too close to the windows."

I saw the hail as it came across the lake, ice globs smashing into the water like bullets from invisible guns. Then *thuck thuck thuck* up the hill and *boom boom boom* on the roof. A half-dozen Scouts took shelter under the pines across the way. Until the hail let up, they were stuck there. More Scouts filed into the dining hall, random teen boys from different troops all across camp.

There was lightning, followed by another loud *crack,* and then the power went out. The boys screamed happily.

We brought out candles from the kitchen and lanterns from storage as the hail diminished and the rain began to fall in force. Several Scouts were swinging flashlights around the dark interior of the dining hall, playing lightsabers. There was too much disarray to get a proper count.

I watched as the raindrops scooted sideways along the panes of glass, the way they do in car washes when you're in between the blowers. There was a *crackling* as a tree across the lake snapped and fell over.

There were maybe two hundred boys in the mess hall by the time Ian returned. He pushed against the wind, through the side door, and stood there, panting. "There are tents everywhere," he said. He still didn't know if his mother was okay, I realized. I think he was in shock. "This summer is cursed," he whispered, and disappeared into the kitchen.

I found a group of Scouts to sit with. They'd arranged themselves in a circle around a lantern on the floor. They were younger, around thirteen, fourteen.

"There was lightning . . ."

"If there is a tornado, are we really safe in here?" one of the boys asked.

"Oh yeah," I lied. "This place was built to withstand even the strongest tornado." White lies are permitted at camp. Whenever a Scout spotted a snake in the lake, we assured them that it couldn't get through the snake nets around the swimming area, so they weren't too afraid to go back in. But in my head I created a detailed play where the tornado came down and the walls exploded into a million splinters and then the churning wind swept us up into the black.

"What's it like being on staff?" another boy asked.

"It's fun," I said. "Mostly fun. You get to see all the skits again each week."

"Did someone really die here last week?"

"Not here. But yes, a staff member died," I said.

"What happened to him?"

"I don't know."

Across the way I saw Lauren enter from the kitchen. She mouthed "What the fuck" as she looked at the refugees gathered on the floor.

"It's crazy, right?" I said, walking over.

"I can't stop crying about Mike, and now this," she said.

"Ian thinks we're cursed."

"Mike dying is terrible, but could you imagine if we lost a kid?"

Just then, a bolt of lightning flashed outside, a few hundred feet away. The younger Scouts screamed. Nobody was joking now.

"There are still troops out there," she said. "All the troops in the Back Forty."

For a moment we simply stared into the storm. "Any blacksnake sightings this week?" I asked, my attempt at changing the subject. There was absolutely nothing we could do for the Scouts outside.

"Oh yeah, the boys keep bringing them in," she said. "But I release them before the Pipestone elders come to collect. They're pissed at me, but until they let me run, they're not getting any snakes for the ceremony. Not from me."

"Fuck 'em," I said.

On Wednesday nights Lucas assumed his role
as camp chaplain for a nondenominational service
at an open-air chapel near the amphitheater
on the shore of Lake Donahey.

"Helmet Head!" That was Ronald, the cook. He was standing at the swinging kitchen door. "Come help me."

I followed him into the kitchen and he pointed to the walk-in freezer. "I think the power's going to be out for a while. All the ice cream is melting. Why don't you take it out to the boys."

Ronald kept the ice cream in cylindrical cardboard containers about the size of a footstool. I looked around for bowls, but he just handed me a stack of spoons. "They can eat it out of the tubs," he said.

One by one I delivered tubs of melting ice cream to groups of Scouts huddled together on the concrete floor. Cookie dough, Rocky Road, chocolate, and vanilla. I gave everyone a spoon, and after a minute it was silent inside. Nobody cared about the thunder; nobody counted out how close the storm was. All of our collective anxiety fell away as we dug into the ice cream. I helped myself to the cookie dough, spoonful after spoonful. We wiped our hands on our jeans, our mouths, our sleeves, and everything was sticky and boys laughed to know how mad their mothers would be if they could see them now.

Ronald watched from the door, smiling. He caught me looking and scowled, then walked away.

The power stayed off until eleven o'clock that night. By then, the storm had gone and the troops had returned to their camps, to reassemble their tents. Nobody died that night. A couple Scouts were injured running to the dining hall. One older staff member was taken to the hospital after slipping on a trail and cutting his arm open on a tree branch. But we all survived.

I attended Lucas Taylor's vespers service that week. On Wednesday nights Lucas assumed his role as camp chaplain for a nondenominational service at an open-air chapel near the amphitheater on the shore of Lake Donahey. It was not mandatory for staff. My friends remained in their tents smoking cigarettes and listening to Ace of Base. But I felt an urge to go that week. When I was younger, I attended a private Christian school. The older women who ran the preschool would tell us the most wonderful stories about redemption and forgiveness and

He finished his service before the sun set

and I helped put the pews away.

love for your fellow man. And there were always happy songs played with an acoustic guitar. That's what I wanted right then. I needed a reminder that people were good.

Two chaplains-in-training were setting up as I arrived. I helped them bring down the wood pews from the loft. We placed the pews in four rows facing the lake and then set the podium up front. Scouts arrived in small groups and chose their seats. At five minutes before eight, I spotted Lucas coming down the trail, his guitar slung to one side like a holstered rifle. He saw me and gave a curious smile.

"Renner," he said. "I thought I might see you here."

I sat on the grassy slope behind the chapel and watched as Lucas tuned his guitar, allowing time for the stragglers. The pews filled up and then others joined me on the hill or stood leaning on the chapel supports. Lucas looked out at the crowd and I could see he was touched by the turnout. He began the service with a version of the song "The Flower That Shattered the Stone," which had been popularized by John Denver. I was unfamiliar with the song, but I loved its message: how small, beautiful things can still win out in the end. He sang the second verse in Japanese—I think he had studied there at one time.

"My Seven Ranges family has had a very difficult week," he said, and his eyes found me in the audience. "I wasn't sure that I could be here tonight. But I'm glad I came. Because this is by far the largest group I've ever seen at vespers. I forget how music and our love of God can comfort our spirits in difficult times. Let us pray."

Lucas said a short prayer. I watched as everyone bowed their heads and closed their eyes. When he was done, he let the quiet expand. We all sat there, looking out at the water. Lucas turned to look, too. We were all so quiet that a blue heron settled on the shore and looked back at us. Someone laughed, startling the bird, and it flew away.

"We tend to go through our day and not think about the nature that is all around us," Lucas said. "But it's always there, patiently waiting for us to return to it. Look at that view. Isn't it beautiful? Aren't we lucky to see it? Let us remember to never take it for granted. Not for one day."

He strummed his guitar again and sang "Hosanna." I joined in on the refrain, even though I'd never had much of a voice for singing. But it felt good to try.

He finished his service before the sun set and I helped put the pews away.

"Walk with me back to Admin," Lucas said when I was done.

I followed him down the path that led to the front of camp.

"I'm sorry I couldn't tell you what was going on with Tommy and Mike," he said.

"It's okay," I replied. "I still don't understand what happened. There're a couple different stories going around. I heard Tommy got into a fight with Mike, that he got kicked out for having a beer."

We continued on for a moment while Lucas considered how to respond. Finally he said, "It's not my place to go into detail. It's not my story to tell, you know? But what happened was not Tommy's fault. Tommy was the victim."

"Is he coming back to camp?"

"No," said Lucas.

"Did Mike really kill himself?"

Lucas sighed. "I don't know. I think so."

"Do you think Mike was the one that burned down the old Trading Post?"

"Possible. I don't think we'll ever know for sure. But don't repeat that."

I remembered something then and fished around in my pockets for a second. I found what I was looking for and then stopped on the trail. "Hey, Lucas, check it out."

I waved my hand in the air with a flourish like a proper magician. I had learned to place a card behind my hand, held in place by my first finger and pinky. I went to swing it around to make it seem like the card had appeared out of thin air, but when I tried it, the card went flying into the woods.

"Damn," I said.

But it made Lucas laugh. "Keep practicing," he said.

When I got back to my tent that night, I was surprised to find the spare bed had a sleeping bag on it. And there was another backpack on the floor.

A boy came in, pushing the flap to one side. His hair was wet and he had a towel over his shoulder. He had pale blue eyes and high cheekbones. He reminded me of the actor Jonathan Brandis.

"Hello, there," I said.

"Oh, hey," he said. "Scooter told me to take the bunk. I'm the new CIT."

I shook his hand. "James Renner," I said.

"Eddie," he replied. "Eddie Rambler."

now

I want to tell you about my daughter, because she was the one that put me back on a path to recovery in 2023. Laine is ten. She has cinnamon-colored hair, a recessive genetic holdover from great-grandparents. She's my artist. She dances barefoot and takes small roles in community plays and sings with a choir in Cleveland. She conducts daily experiments in the kitchen. She's constantly making slime or brownies-in-a-bowl. When she was born, she breathed in amniotic fluid on the way out and came out blue, and the nurse brought her over to a table on the other end of the delivery room and tried to fix her fast. I followed her while the other doctors took care of Julie.

"She's not breathing," the nurse said. She fished through a drawer and came out with a thin plastic hose and shoved it far up my daughter's nose, and then she squeezed the suction and a bunch of stuff came out. Laine coughed and cried and started to breathe and her skin turned from blue to pink. The nurse sighed with relief.

"Is she okay?" I asked.

"I don't think it was long enough for brain damage," she said. What a frightening thing to hear in the first moment of life. They kept Laine in the NICU for a couple days and she was fine. Still, there was a part of me that worried until she started walking, until she said her first words. I think about that memory a lot. It's a reminder that I should never take her for granted.

And while she is only ten, and my son, Casey, is fifteen, and Julie is a woman of a certain age, Laine is often the most emotionally perceptive of our bunch. Both Casey and Julie are neurodivergent, as they say these days, though it would take a while for you to notice if you were in the same room. Casey's autism expresses itself through his singular focus, his knowledge of music instruments, a need for routine, and his penchant for whistling to soothe himself. Julie can't make eye contact when she's upset, and she does the whistling thing, too. Her diagnosis came late and doesn't matter much in hindsight. She's blunt and sometimes that gets her into trouble. And maybe it's hard for her to express herself emotionally, but I always know where I stand with her. She's incapable of being passive-aggressive. She's a wonderful partner. Laine's the perceptive one. So, naturally, she was the one who caught me sneaking vodka from the cabinet.

"I thought you weren't drinking alcohol," she said with a decidedly grown-up look of disappointment.

"Ah," I said. "Right. I suppose I'm not modeling good behavior."

"No, you're not."

I could see my own childhood confusion in her eyes and that hurt most of all. When I was her age, my mother started going to AA and I didn't understand why. What was so bad about drinking that you needed to go to a secret club to stop? And whenever I asked, the answer was always different. Sometimes she explained that she wasn't an alcoholic, but she was going because my stepfather was an alcoholic and she needed support. As I got older, she told me that it was because she had issues with drugs and AA was there for that, too. But eventually she told me most of the truth, that she was drunk or high whenever I wasn't there for our every-other-weekend visit. She cleaned herself up whenever she had me and then went back into the bottle, be it booze or pills, until I came again. We were close, see? Before my parents split when I was three, I was my mother's shadow. And someone had taken her shadow away. You do what you can to numb yourself to that. No judgment here.

I'm making things confusing for my daughter and why? My family isn't broken. What did I have to complain about, really?

So I stopped again. But I knew if I wanted to quit for good, I had to fundamentally change those stubborn habits of my mind.

I first heard about Jonathan Lubecky by way of the Maura Murray case—the young woman who went missing in New Hampshire, in 2004—the subject of my book *True Crime Addict*. Maura's boyfriend, Bill Rausch, was a major in the army and a rising star in the world of Veterans Affairs when my reporting uncovered claims of sexual assault and harassment that led to him being indicted for felony sex abuse in DC. (He pleaded guilty to a lesser charge of misdemeanor assault in 2023.) Jonathan was one of several soldiers who reached out during my investigation and we exchanged emails every other month or so. I was intrigued by the work Jonathan was doing in Washington. He was working for MAPS, lobbying Congress to change laws related to the use of psychedelics for therapy.

It's a five-hour drive to DC from Akron if you take the toll roads. I drove out one evening in February to meet Jonathan in person at the Silver Diner in the historic Navy Yard district. He arrived late, in need of a cigarette. But soon he'd settled into the booth and ordered some fries.

Turns out, Jonathan grew up not far from me, in Brecksville, Ohio, an upper-class suburb of Cleveland. But he never really fit in with that crowd. He liked to run around the woods with a rifle, he liked to work on cars. He found himself at marine bootcamp nine days after graduation.

He worked as an air crewman on C-130 transport planes for a while, and lived in Japan for a year. Then, after the attacks on 9/11, Jonathan joined the National Guard in North Carolina. He wanted to fly helicopters in Iraq so he joined an artillery unit to qualify. They sent him to Balad, Iraq. One day he was in a porta-potty when a mortar came in and blew it up. Jonathan survived with a traumatic brain injury.

When he returned Stateside in 2006, Jonathan did not adjust well to civilian life. He still lived close enough to Fort Bragg to hear the sound of artillery as they trained new recruits. Every time there was an explosion, he jumped into action. His body was still in combat mode, still hypervigilant, waiting for the sound of the next incoming mortar. It was like a muscle he didn't know how to relax. When he ventured out to a restaurant, he'd find himself reaching for his rifle on the way out. In the field a soldier never went anywhere without his rifle. Without his weapon he felt vulnerable all the time.

Jonathan felt his mind breaking, a piece at a time. It got bad around the holidays and one night he went out to a bar in Raleigh to drink away his anxiety. It was Christmas Eve and at midnight he heard the tolling of the church bells for midnight mass. He walked to the church with the intention of confessing his fears and asking for help, but it was full to capacity and he was turned away at the door. So he went home, opened a bottle of vodka, loaded his 9mm Beretta, aimed the barrel at his temple, and pulled the trigger. It was a squib load. The bullet didn't exit. A malfunction.

"It took me a bit to figure out that I wasn't dead," he said. "And that only made me more upset. I couldn't even kill myself right."

After that, he sought help at the Womack Army Medical Center, where a doctor gave him six Xanax and told him to give his guns to his neighbor.

That was his first attempt. He tried to kill himself four more times over the next eight years. After the last time, while he was recovering at yet another hospital, an intern who'd taken the time to actually read through his full VA file wrote a message on a piece of paper and told him to keep it in his pocket until he got out. On it was written: *google MDMA PTSD.* That's how he learned about MAPS.

He applied to their program and was accepted into a drug trial that was taking place in a house in Mount Pleasant, South Carolina. Since it was a scientific study, some of the participants were given placebos. He didn't know for sure if he was one of the lucky ones actually getting MDMA. He was given a green pill to swallow and told to lie down on a bed. A therapist was stationed on either side of the bed and he was told to talk about anything related to his trauma, however mundane.

"Nobody tells you this shit takes forty-five minutes to kick in," he said. "So I was there for, like, twenty minutes, and I figured, well, I got the placebo." But then, a short time later, he realized he had completely lost all concept of time. "Time was passing, but I didn't know if it was five seconds, five minutes, or five hours."

"What was the weather like in Iraq?" one of the therapists asked him.

Jonathan began to describe the unbearable heat in the "Suck," as they call it. One story led to another and soon he was reliving that day when a bomb nearly killed him. For the first time he could experience that memory objectively, without fear.

"There were no more nightmares after that," he said.

When he returned to DC, Jonathan could not stop talking about the benefits of MDMA therapy and how it ended the compulsion he had to die by suicide. He was a changed man. Word got around to journalists. He was featured in articles and then documentaries on the use of psychedelics to treat trauma. He had an affable personality and an ear for storytelling. He was the perfect spokesman for this experiment and eventually Rick Doblin, himself, noticed.

"What if we pay you to do this?" he asked Jonathan in 2018. Since then, Jonathan has been employed by MAPS, where he does media analysis, political intelligence, education, and lobbying. Because Jonathan is a marine, conservative politicians listen to him.

Republican congressman Dan Crenshaw keeps an apartment in his building and one day Jonathan caught him in the elevator. On the way down he gave his pitch on the need for psychedelic studies to help military veterans. In April 2023, Representative Crenshaw led a bipartisan effort to urge the National Institutes of Health to include active-duty service members in their research into psychedelic therapies.

Jonathan credits MDMA with saving his life and for showing him the beauty and joy in the world that he had lost the ability to see after his deployment. He's on a mission to help others experience the same awakening. And not just in the United States. Earlier this year he traveled to Ukraine, where he volunteered his time organizing the transport of food and weapons to the soldiers on the front. But his real goal was to scope out the territory for his next project—setting up a psychedelic therapy clinic there to treat soldiers suffering with PTSD from combat.

"I want to battle-test MDMA in Ukraine," he said. "If we can show that MDMA-assisted therapy can treat PTSD, to the point that soldiers are willing to return to the front lines, I think that's when things will really change. We're losing so many of our men to psychological trauma. But what if we don't have to? What if they can come back?"

My guide into the world of psychedelics was an army vet named Mac, who kept an apartment in DC. He, too, was a subject in the MDMA therapy studies, but was not a therapist. He asked not to be identified further. This one was strictly off the books.

Mac's apartment was not much bigger than a dorm room, just enough space for him and a dog named Calliope. The living room was narrow, room for a couch and a TV. Mac had me lie on the couch and surrounded me with thick blankets. Calliope came around with a tennis ball in her mouth, so Mac and I took turns throwing it across the apartment for her to fetch.

"Rule number one," said Mac in a stern voice, "once we begin, do not attempt to open the door to my balcony. If you try it, I will physically restrain you from doing so. Okay?"

"Okay." He didn't have to explain further. That balcony was high enough to get the job done if the idea of suicide sounded tempting during a psychotic break.

"Rule number two, cry if you need to cry. It's part of the process. We are in a partnership for the next several hours. I'm here to help, you're here to heal. Whatever you tell me stays with me. Understood?"

"Understood."

"Good." He walked to the fridge. He returned with a chocolate bar he purchased in Oakland that was infused with psilocybin. It comes in sleek packaging, with a human brain floating over a field of mushrooms on the front.

The chocolate bar is dosed by the square. You can eat one square to microdose. You won't trip. Things won't begin to melt. But you might feel lighter throughout the day. If you want a true experience, what they call a threshold dose, half a bar is recommended. Taking an entire bar is considered a "heroic" dose and should only be done by experienced psychonauts. Mac gave me half the bar and I settled down for the wait. Like edibles of other sorts, psilocybin takes a while for the body to metabolize. So we watched Nate Bargatze clips on YouTube for a while and I tossed the ball for Calliope. Every fifteen minutes Mac would step onto the balcony to vape from two separate pens—one full of marijuana, the other nicotine.

After about forty-five minutes I asked for more chocolate. He told me to wait another half hour. Thirty minutes later, I still wasn't feeling the effects, so he gave me another quarter of the bar.

"Buckle up," he said.

He played music on the TV then. MAPS has a playlist for psychedelic therapy on Spotify. Tribal music, mostly, like the *Pure Moods* CD my mom used to play all the time. I lay back on the couch and closed my eyes.

The first thing I noticed was that I began to feel pleasantly warm. It reminded me of Oxy, that feeling of being wrapped in a thermal blanket, but much more gentle and complete. A Native American medicine man began singing and suddenly I could see the music. Temporary synesthesia is a common side effect of psilocybin, and many people have reported the ability to "see" sound. But having experienced it, I don't think that's a truly accurate description of what is going on. It's not really sight that I experienced. I wasn't really "seeing." I was interpreting the sound as images in my mind, sure, and my brain seemed to be encoding that data as visuals. But . . . look. When you smell pine trees, what do you see in your mind? They say smell is the greatest sense-link to memory. So maybe when you smell pine trees, you recall a time in your life that was special to you that was encoded with that particular smell. The backyard hideout at your favorite grandparents' house. Or the fragrance of the cedar closet where you would hide when your father was drunk and looking for a fight. For me, when I smell pine, I recall that path that leads away from Lake Donahey and meanders up toward Handicraft. Is that an image? Not really. It's the idea of an image. Almost like another sense entirely. Like a memory. That's what they mean when they say you can see sound.

I saw myself standing on a great, open plain under a starless sky and the medicine man's music was pulling something into existence above me. I felt the music sweep through me like a ray of sunlight through a prism, the song filtering through each of the subjective experiences of my individual life and exiting from me as this . . . this artwork creature in the sky. The creature I was calling into being above me was billowy. Symmetrical. As the song continued, it grew in size until I could see that it was made of a kind of heavy fabric, like a quilt. And it was alive. It was an alive thing. And it resembled, in ways, a cuttlefish—that species of squid with membranous frills around its underbelly.

I saw, or I imagined that I saw, two beings on this plain with me, witnesses to my creation. To them, this was another fireworks show, perhaps. This was the world of such things, the world of forms. They were beings that might look at something like this fabric cuttlefish and understand how it projects from the events of my life. And in that way I hope they were impressed.

"We should talk about your trauma now," said Mac.

I opened my eyes. Mac was leaning against the glass doors that led to the balcony, to the choice of annihilation. Mac, like the medicine man, played an important role. He was the highwayman, the Walk-and-Talk Man, a guide between two worlds. And I saw then what great toll it took for him to do this for us damaged people. He had to remain anchored in both universes.

"I'm ready," I said.

"You should recall a traumatic event and you should tell me about it. It's safe here. Tell me what you see."

The whole purpose of this side quest was to make sense of what we went through at Seven Ranges and how it shaped my friends and me as adults. I willed myself to remember the sweat lodge behind the Indian Shower House. To remember that man—Jim Mills—and what happened to us at the end of that summer. But that's not what my mind did.

I saw nothing of Pipestone or the hills around Lake Donahey.

I was in the kitchen of the farmhouse where I lived as a child, the one in Ravenna, before we moved again for second grade. I had not thought of this place in many years. I was standing beside myself, beside myself as a five-year-old boy with an overly round head. My stepmother had picked me up from kindergarten and we had just come through the back door and I was angry. Angry that I could not see my mother.

"I hate it here!" I shouted.

Linda spun around and struck me. Punched me. Hard enough to send me backward, off my feet, sliding across the tiled floor.

And though I was not the boy, not anymore, I could read that boy's mind because it was my own. I felt his sudden realization: *My dad has no idea who this woman really is. He's made a terrible mistake.*

"What do you see?" asked Mac.

"My stepmother," I said.

"Wait," he said. "Wait for it."

And then I saw the moment from a higher dimension. I mean that *literally*. And I will try to describe it, but I don't think we have the language for it. Consider a two-dimensional world. If we lived in a two-dimensional world, we would be stick figures on a page of paper. And if we were to rise up one dimension, we could stare down at ourselves and see a pair of shears cut through the paper, cut through our existence, ending who we are. I saw the moment she first struck me, the twenty seconds of it all. I saw it as a cube. Or maybe you would call it a tesseract, since a cube is still three-dimensional. And I watched as that quilt creature, that monstrosity of a cuttlefish, began to wrap its blue-and-white tentacles around that event, which was static in this higher dimension. Its tentacles wrapped around all the moments in that sad scene. And the tentacles grew in size and number, until all I could see was the monster itself and it had entirely devoured my memory and my pain.

I did cry then. Not out of any sadness, but out of awe. I felt that memory detach from my being, from having any influence on my ego or my idea of myself. I felt free. Amazingly, wonderfully free.

"It eats memories," I said.

"Yes," said Mac.

I won't bore you with the other visions that came on its tale. But this trip went on for some time, hours, days, years, eons. Around midnight Mac deemed me safe enough to venture back to my hotel and he called an Uber for me. I flew through the capital city in the back of a Kia, the streetlights trailing behind us, listening to K-pop.

When I was back at the hotel, I felt that the more profound visions were finished. I felt I was safe, alone. But then I made one very rookie mistake—I went into the bathroom and looked in the mirror. They warn you to avoid mirrors.

I saw myself objectively for the first time in my existence. That is the power of psychedelics. They separate us from our ego and that can be a very frightening thing, because it's something that must be faced with complete humility. What I saw was a middle-aged man, not the young man I see in my mind as the representation of the idea of James Renner, but the man I am today.

"Look at all the gray hair," I said.

I stepped closer and angled my head so I could see the white hair that had grown up from my temples. I ran my fingers through my hair, my fingertips tingling with electricity. I stared at myself for many minutes or perhaps only a second. I wanted more. I wanted to see me from every angle. And so I went to the makeup mirror, that round mirror they put on the countertops in fancy hotels so women can see their face in high definition. Bad fucking idea. That mirror told a different story altogether. I was older, so old. Seventy at least. I could see where the elasticity of my skin had given up around my eyes. I could see liver spots and a thinning crown, barely a wisp of hair remained. I didn't want this one to be true.

Maybe I could see the truth if I put the mirrors together, I thought. And so I picked up the makeup mirror and turned it around so

I could see myself in the larger mirror behind me, reflected through the smaller one. The two mirrors divided myself into four separate reflections, doppelgangers, reverse images of the same person looking back at himself. I became recursive. It was James Renners all the way down and I forgot which one was really me.

Don't panic, I told myself. *You can find your way out.*

I love you, I told myself.

I hate you, I told myself.

I forgive you, I said.

I'll never forget, I said.

After a long, terrible confinement, I decided that I was the image in the big mirror, the one with the salt-and-pepper hair. And once I made that decision, I was able to set the other mirror down and return to myself.

I avoided the bathroom for the rest of the night.

When I woke, I was utterly unaware of the time. It felt like the middle of the night still, but I was rested. No hangover. No nausea. But it was completely black in the room. I looked at the clock. It said 10:30. My first thought was that I had slept through an entire day and it was now the following evening. But I remembered that I had pulled the heavy curtains shut tight the day before. I'd slept late, but not that late.

I spent the day walking around DC, from the White House to the Washington Monument to the Lincoln Memorial. My mind was quiet! For the first time in so many years, my mind was quiet. It was open and hungry for new information, new adventures, unhindered by petty worries and useless anxieties. I took my time walking over the memorial grounds, in awe of the architecture and the audacity of the Founding Fathers and the gambles they'd taken to secure their place in history. And I felt kinship for the people I passed on the lawn. If we could only remember always that we were all a part of the same big thing.

That night I did not crave a drink.

then

I was serving slushies at the Trading Post when the cannons went off. Three in a row. *Boom. Boom. Boom.*

"Oh, shit, what now?" said Norman.

"I'll close down, you guys go," said Mark, coming through the door to the souvenir shop. Since he was such a slight man, Mark was excused from emergency calls.

Norman, Trey, and I jumped through the concession window and shot off down the road toward the dining hall. When we rounded the hill, I saw Ben standing at the parade grounds by the cannon. He waved to us and then pointed to Waterfront. My heart plummeted. That could mean only one thing—a body search.

"Fuck," said Trey. We ran faster.

By the time we got to Waterfront, I was out of breath. We were among twenty or so staff members who'd answered the call. The Waterfront director, a guy named Brandon, quickly briefed us.

"One tag on the board," he said. "A Scout from Mingo Mesa, Troop 19. His swim buddy returned to their campsite, but he did not. Last seen in the intermediate section about thirty minutes ago. We'll do a sweep. Go, go, go!"

Waterfront was divided into three swim areas. There was the shallow end for nonswimmers; the intermediate area in between two docks, where Scouts could still touch the sandy bottom; and the deep end for advanced swimmers. We jogged down the wooden docks and jumped into the middle section. We formed a tight line and began walking forward, reaching out with our feet for the boy's body.

I don't know if you've ever had the displeasure of searching for

We formed a tight line and began walking forward,
reaching out with our feet for the boy's body.

a dead child's body. But it's a job that you have to perform well, but one where you don't actually want to succeed. If he was in the water, we had to find him. But our only reward was anguish. I didn't want to find a body under the water. I didn't want to be the one to provide the ultimate answer.

We continued searching for an excruciating ten minutes, all of us aware that if the boy had gone under, he'd been down too long for resuscitation. I was also very conscious of the fact that I was likely the most qualified of the bunch to administer CPR if we did find him and I'd have to try.

But then the boy came running down the trail from the Back Forty, wearing his towel like a cape. "I'm sorry!" he shouted. "Sorry!" He ran over, got his tag, and placed it on the out-of-water board, while we all watched in silence. "I'm sorry!" he shouted again, then ran away.

"I need a smoke," said Trey. I was dripping wet and needed to change, but I walked with him and Norman back to their tent in Peninsula. The mood among the staff had grown dark since the beginning of summer, when these hangouts were full of harmless ribbing and dirty jokes. In the span of two weeks, a member of our staff had died, another was simply gone, a tornado had nearly destroyed camp, and we'd helped search for a boy's body. A gloom had settled over everyone's fun. And I felt entirely too grown-up.

"Did they have a funeral for Mike?" I asked, sitting on their floor.

"It was last Saturday," said Trey, taking a drag on his cigarette. "I went with some of the others who knew him. They brought a bus for us. It was open casket. Just a line of people walking past his coffin. Then they brought us back before dark." He turned on the radio and found "Cotton Eye Joe."

"This summer is biblical," Norman said, sitting on his bed.

"I kept thinking I'd be the one that found the boy in the water," I said. "Like, I kept waiting to step on his head or something."

"I know what you mean," Norman replied.

"What do you think will happen next?"

"A plague of locust," said Trey.

"Maybe camp really is cursed," I said. "All the Pipestone stuff . . . old men dressing up and painting their skin red. There's got to be a hundred Indians buried on this land. Maybe they've had enough."

"Oh, that's a pleasant thought," said Norman. "That'll help me sleep tonight. Thanks for that."

"You're going to finish your Pipestone, though, right?" asked Trey.

"I don't know."

"If you get your fifth, they'll let you cross the road. You have to see the ISH at least."

"The ISH?"

"Indian Shower House."

"Yeah," said Norman. "The leaders sit around naked eating spaghetti for an hour before they put their paint on."

"Gross."

"If you complete your Pipestone," said Trey, "we can go spy on the fourth-year ceremony the last week of camp. I gotta hear that masturbation speech again."

"It's weird, right?" I said. "That grown men are so concerned about teenage boys masturbating?"

"I think it's just about tradition," said Norman. "Pipestone is like seventy years old and nobody wants to change it. Some parts of the speech are outdated, but it's more about keeping the tradition of the ceremony alive." Then he added: "I hope."

On Thursday night that week, the staff was told to report to Admin directly after Retreat and to dress for the real world. Jeans and tees. There was a line of minivans waiting for us when we arrived. I took a seat next to Trey and Norman. In light of the events of the recent weeks, Buckeye Council was treating us to a night out.

They took us to Belden Village Mall, outside Canton. If you weren't around in 1995, the thing you should know is that the malls were always busy. We didn't have Amazon or Grubhub. The Internet, for those of us who had it, was mostly text based. There was no real way to order shit online. The malls were our Amazon—it was the one location where you could get anything from candy to a new CD to a nice suit. The best video games were still in the arcades. And if you wanted to see a new movie, you went to the cinema, which was usually near the food court. It was also the best place to meet chicks from other schools, since Insta and Snapchat were distant dreams.

I don't remember who came up with the idea for the contest. But we all played. The contest was simple: Who could get the most phone numbers from cute girls before we left? We split up. Divide and conquer, I guess. I felt bad gathering phone numbers I had no intention of using, so my approach with girls was to explain to them about the contest and tell them it was better that I win than some jerk. Every time I saw Trey across the way, he was talking up a group of smiling teen girls. He had a confidence the rest of us lacked. My stomach twisted in complicated jealousy. Jealous that he could get that attention. But also jealous of the girls.

I stopped playing the game then and just walked in and out of stores. I bumped into Lucas at Sam Goody. He was waiting in line at the register to buy a CD. I had terrible taste back then and my CD collection consisted mostly of television soundtracks. My favorite was the soundtrack to *Quantum Leap*. I liked to play it at night as I drifted off to sleep. While we waited, Lucas and I both spotted the sleight of hand that happened beside us. Lucas, after all, was a master of sleight of hand. A young well-dressed man in line in front of Lucas pointed to a CD on the shelf behind the counter, so the woman at the register went to get it. When her back was turned, the man snatched a toy off the counter and put it in his pocket. It was a little troll or something. Probably cost two bucks. It was done with practiced ease.

Lucas looked to me to see if I'd noticed. I nodded. He just sighed. "It's not like camp out here," he said.

Later, they let us choose between two movies: *Apollo 13* or this weird sci-fi movie starring Russell Crowe called *Virtuosity* about an artificial intelligence constructed from the minds of a hundred serial

killers that becomes self-aware, a real '90s-era popcorn extravaganza.
I chose *Virtuosity* and sat beside Trey.

"You get a lot of phone numbers?" I asked.

He showed me a sheet of paper with at least twenty phone numbers on it, written in girlish bright colors. Then he crumpled it up and
tossed it into the dark. That made me smile.

It was late by the time we returned to camp. On the way home I
watched the lights of Belden Village fall away. The minivan turned onto
the highway and then a state route and then into the backcountry of
Columbiana County, and the lights of civilization disappeared entirely
and it was dark all around. It struck me again how like another world
Seven Ranges was. This was the way to Narnia, to Fantasia. I wondered which world was more real.

We gathered on the scoutmaster's patio when we got back. We
reclined in chairs under the tarp awning and there was still an air of
frivolity among the crew. We'd had fun, damn it. We could still have
fun. And there was also a general relief of having returned to camp, to
the place we tried so hard to make wonderful for hundreds of Scouts
each week.

Lucas stood and raised his hand in a Scout salute. Everyone hushed
immediately.

"I want to tell you about something I saw out there tonight," he
began. "I was in a store with Renner, buying a CD. And I saw a man
steal a toy. Right in the open. Like he'd done it a hundred times. And
he showed no shame, no fear. He almost looked bored. That's what
the world is like out there. But camp is different. I think we need to
remember that. We've built something special here. Seven Ranges is
as close a thing to Utopia as I can think of. I know it's been a rough
summer. But we still haven't lost what's great about this place. We've
made it a world where we're always looking after each other, pushing
each other to be our best selves, keeping those children safe, giving
them such great memories."

Lucas looked to me as I brushed away a tear. *Summer would be over soon* was what I was thinking. We could not stay here forever. None of us.

"We'll take it with us," he said as if reading my mind. "And it will make that outside world just a little better."

That Friday night I duct-taped the bottom of my jeans to my boots and put on my long flannel shirt and then jogged to Admin, where I joined the group of fifth-year Pipestone candidates waiting to cross the road. I was surprised to see Lauren waiting with the first-year Scouts, the lone woman among their ranks—the first in Pipestone history. She saw me, waved, then walked over.

"Congratulations," I said. "How'd you do it?"

"They realized they would never get another blacksnake as long as I work here and I'm coming back next summer. So they reluctantly said yes."

"Well done."

"Thank you. But now I can't, like, trip on the trail or give up halfway through or they'll never let another girl in."

"You'll be fine. Keep a little distance between yourself and the person in front of you."

"Right on." The first-year candidates started to cross the road then, and she ran over to join them. I was worried for her, to tell the truth. If the Pipestone elders were mad, the best way to get back at her would be to beat the shit out of her on the trail. But then again, Lauren could hold her own.

Eventually they came for the fifth-year Scouts. And I crossed the road as a candidate for the last time.

now

"Eddie," I said. "Come here."

It was early. I'd just pulled into his driveway, in my Subaru. His daughter, Sarah, hopped in with her backpack and a handful of sourdough pretzels. Laine sat beside her, ready for school.

Eddie came off his front porch, over to my window. He wore a wool ivy cap because it was sprinkling. "Morning," he said.

With a rather impressive flourish, I made a business card appear in my hand. Jonathan Lubecky's phone number was on it. "Please call this guy. They're still doing VA studies on psychedelics. I bet you could get in."

"Sweet," he said, pocketing the card. "Thank you."

I waved and pulled away.

I still felt amazing. Something fundamental inside me had changed. A piece of who I had been was no more. Maybe I hadn't killed my ego entirely, but I had killed a piece of me, for sure. And I didn't miss it. I didn't miss the call to the bottle. I felt that even if I drank again, it could never be with the same limitless desire. That great, poisonous vine of craving in my soul, grown from a seed of simple need, was dead.

I was feeling like myself again. And that was good timing. Because it was time to investigate how Mike Klingler became Mike Klingler. The last thing I needed was a monkey on my shoulder for that dark journey.

I wanted to understand why Klingler had gone crazy. I wanted to know if he really did kill himself. I wanted to know if he was the arsonist of Seven Ranges. I had only the end of his story. But where did it really begin?

I drove out to Beach City one weekend in April. It's a forty-five-minute drive from Akron, but it's as far from the city as you can get. Amish buggies still roll down Main Street on a Saturday afternoon—there's a hitching post in front of the Dollar General. The outlying roads are sparsely populated by farmers too busy working their fields to pay much attention to the upkeep of their homesteads, clapboard shacks, dirty kid toys left out on overgrown lawns, animal-print blankets for curtains. At night the local hooligans gather at Machan's Rock to smoke pot and to paint graffiti on the cave entrance, which was blasted shut in the 1950s after a guy died inside.

Driving through these far-flung Ohio hamlets, my mind, unprompted, imagined what it would be like to live there. I grew up in a town like this and maybe that's why I feel a pull to return to similar places. There's a real temptation to drop it all, the never-ending money chase, the upkeep of a house with a mortgage, the politics of modern-day publishing, to give it up and to come to a place like Beach City and disappear into it. A double-wide at the trailer park here runs about $7,000. I could spend my days inside reading old books, avoiding humanity. Unplug. No TikTok, no Facebook. Maybe install a landline and ditch the cell phone entirely. Get an old TV set with an antenna and limit myself to five fuzzy channels that still play commercials. If that doesn't at least sound tempting, I don't understand you.

This is where Mike Klingler grew up, in an A-frame house on a narrow road in Beach City, which is not a city at all and has no beach. His parents are old now, but still live in the same house. They weren't home, so I stopped next door to speak with Janette Weisgarber, the woman who called the police the day Mike died. She talked to me on her stoop while a grandkid played inside. She told me the Klinglers had left that morning, possibly to get breakfast at the Hardee's in Strasburg, which was their weekend routine.

"My daughter just moved in next door," Janette said, pointing to a new home on the other end of her property. "We gave her some land in exchange for taking care of us when we get old, you know? She and her husband built that themselves. It's a garage-aminium."

"'A garage-aminium'?"

"Right. Like a condo. Except instead of an extra unit, it has a big garage and the whole thing has concrete flooring."

I said that sounded grand, then steered the conversation back to the topic at hand. "You were here then, when Mike died?"

"I was."

"What do you remember?"

"I remember looking out my window and seeing his feet go flying up into the air." Her house sits about a hundred feet from the Klinglers', and their backyards kind of run together, stretching back to a field. Mike had been partially obscured in the field grass.

"Did you see anybody else out there with him?"

"No," she said. "Only Mike."

"After all these years, what do you think happened?" I asked.

Janette teared up. She shook her head. "I don't know the circumstances that led to it," she said. "And I probably don't want to ever know."

I spared her the details. I waited awhile for the Klinglers to return, but after an hour I left my number in their door and drove home.

Mike's mother, Mary Ann, called later that night. We spoke for some time, reminiscing about her son. She's a nice woman, candid and open to a point.

"Michael's younger brother, Matt, took a trip to Key West not long after he died," she told me. "He had this blue Scouting water bottle, the durable kind. He and his friends took turns putting something meaningful inside. Matt put something in it that reminded him of Michael. They buried it before they left."

It was a nice memory, an act to signify closure to Mike's life. And like Mike, it wouldn't stay buried for long.

"Years later, the bottle surfaced," she said. "Some guy found it and opened it and found an address for one of Matt's friends inside. They got in touch over the Internet. And then he mailed the items back."

"What happened with Mike?" I asked finally.

"As far as what happened at camp, we don't know nothing," she said. "All I know is that they called us to come pick up his things."

"One last question," I said. "Do you remember a man named Jim Mills?"

"I don't," she said.

It seems Mike had been keeping some pretty big secrets from his parents.

Before Mike Klingler became a predator, he was a young man confused about his sexuality. Scouting surely played a significant role in his early sense of self, and, unfortunately, what Scouting—and Pipestone—taught him at that time was that homosexuality was a character flaw that must be kept secret and overcome by sheer force of will.

The Boy Scouts of America's outdated stance on homosexuality was not some aberration, either. The organization has a long history of discrimination and is typically a decade or two behind any liberal societal change.

For instance, some Boy Scout troops remained whites-only twenty years after segregation was declared unconstitutional. In 1974, two Black Scouts wanted to become senior patrol leaders in their Salt Lake City troop. But their troop was sponsored by a local Mormon church. That specific troop required that all senior patrol leaders serve as deacons in the church. And at that time the Latter-day Saints prohibited African Americans from being members of the priesthood. They were stuck in a racially charged catch-22. They could not advance in Scouting because they could not serve as deacons. And they could not serve as deacons because of the color of their skin. When the local paper reached out to the Church of Jesus Christ of Latter-day Saints president, Spencer W. Kimball, he said it would take a revelation from God before the boys would be allowed to serve the Church.

On delicate political issues Boy Scouts HQ has historically taken a leave-it-to-the-locals approach, according to a report by National Public Radio. The BSA leadership typically declines to change policy until they have to, instead leaving each troop across the United States to set the rules for inclusion—unless, of course, you were a woman.

Women were not formally recognized as scoutmasters until 1988, even if they served in such positions in local troops. Catherine Pollard took over Troop 13 in Milford, Connecticut, in 1973, when no one else would step up. She ran the troop, but the Boy Scouts of America refused to accept her application and did not acknowledge her service for another fifteen years.

And while beds got pushed together at summer camps across the United States with a wink and a nudge for those involved, the BSA did not publicly support openly gay Scouts until 2014. In a 1991 position statement, the Boy Scouts of America said, "We believe that homosexual conduct is inconsistent with the requirement in the Scout Oath that a Scout be morally straight and in the Scout Law that a Scout be clean in word and deed, and that homosexuals do not provide a desirable role model for Scouts." I find it incredibly ironic that their defense of discrimination against sexual preference was a law written by a man who was, himself, a closeted homosexual.

In 2000, the Boy Scouts adopted the military's old "don't ask, don't tell" policy, stating, "Boy Scouting makes no effort to discover the sexual orientation of any person." If the Scout was to announce that he was gay, however, his membership would be revoked.

Others felt the organization should set a better example. In 2001, director Steven Spielberg resigned his position on the BSA Advisory Council, saying, "It has deeply saddened me to see the Boy Scouts of America actively and publicly participating in discrimination."

But this was a hundred-year-old institution that preaches the power of tradition and its leaders were reluctant to change Baden-Powell's perfect program. In 2012, the Boy Scouts of America convened a special committee to vote on whether to rescind the ban on gay Scouts. The verdict was unanimous: no fucking way.

Responding to this decision, Richard Ferraro, VP of communication for the Gay and Lesbian Alliance Against Defamation (GLAAD), pointed out to the *New York Times* that the Girl Scouts, the Boys and Girls Clubs, 4-H, and even the military had by then changed their policies to end discrimination based on sexual orientation. "The Boy Scouts of America is one of the last cultural institutions to have discrimination as part of their policy," he said.

In the church basements and community centers, where troop meetings were held every week, things were different. The adults who worked with these closeted gay Scouts noticed something amazing— these boys were no different than the straight ones and carried all the excitement and pride as any other Scout when receiving merit badges and accolades. In March 2013, the Boy Scouts of America posted a survey online for its members. One question went like this: *Tom started in the program as a Tiger Cub and finished every requirement for the Eagle Scout Award at sixteen years of age. At his board of review Tom reveals that he is gay. Is it acceptable or unacceptable for the review board to deny his Eagle Scout award based on that admission?*

Seventy-eight percent felt it was unacceptable. The majority of leaders felt it was time to let the gays in.

Months later, the members of the National Council for the Boy Scouts voted to lift the ban and to begin allowing openly gay Scouts to enter the program beginning January 1, 2014. Things progressed very quickly after that. The following year the Executive Committee voted unanimously to allow openly gay men to serve as leaders. Seventeen-year-old Pascal Tessier became the first openly gay Boy Scout to earn Eagle in 2014. In 2017, they began to allow girl Cub Scout dens, so long as they remained separate from boy dens. Also in 2017, the Boy Scouts of America opened their doors to transgender Scouts. In February of that year, nine-year-old Joe Maldonado of New Jersey became the first transgender Cub Scout. "I am accepted," he said to a reporter for NorthJersey.com. "I'm actually in Boy Scouts!" The first female Eagle Scout, Isabella Tunney, got her Eagle in 2020. By 2022, the rebranded Scouting BSA program had merged the girls' and boys' dens and troops. Now any child who wished to join Scouting could.

This was too much change for the Latter-day Saints to handle. The Mormon Church sponsored over thirty thousand troops and packs across the country, which amounted to around 20 percent of all Boy Scouts, roughly four hundred thousand Scouts. On May 8, 2018, the Church issued a press release in which it declared that it would withdraw its members from the Boy Scouts of America on January 1, 2020. Those children would transfer into a new youth program created to cater to their specific religious beliefs.

"This new approach is intended to help all girls and boys, young women and young men, discover their eternal identity, build character and resilience, develop life skills, and fulfill their divine roles as daughters and sons of God," the Church said.

As they say in the South, bless their hearts.

then

The fifth-year Pipestone ceremony was similar in style to those of the years before: running through the woods, chased by Indians; a short trial inside a clearing surrounded by the skulls of dead animals. For the first time I saw the artifice of it, the embarrassing pageantry. I realized I knew most of the Indians now. Many were older staff members, men I'd spent the summer with. But now, their skin was painted red and I could see half their nut sacks hanging out the sides of their loincloths.

The ceremony ended with one final speech from the chief of Pipestone. This one was not about masturbation, but about service, about giving back to the community. It was also an invitation to return to Seven Ranges and take part in the ceremony as a member of the sacred tribe. Afterward, every Indian came forward to break the fourth wall and shake our hands as equals. Lucas was there, in a black wig. I think he'd always been there, now that I think about it. It's possible he was the Indian that had taken me to the front of the line that very first year. "Hey, bud," he said. We did the secret Pipestone handshake (left hand, pinkies intertwined) and he patted me on the shoulder. "I'm proud of you."

It's hard to not love Pipestone in spite of it all. There is such a sense of belonging, of having survived something extraordinary that not everyone can complete. It rewards perseverance. Because of this, it's easy to overlook the dangers inherent in the program. You feel that you are a part of something older than any one of us. You are keeping tradition alive. Only later, did I think to question why.

More than anything I was excited. By completing my fifth year, I

The fifth-year Pipestone ceremony
was similar in style to those of the years before:
running through the woods, chased by Indians;
a short trial inside a clearing surrounded by
the skulls of dead animals.

now had access to the ISH and I could return the following week to join the tribe as a full-fledged Pipestone apprentice.

The final week of camp was a blur. After eight weeks my job had become routine. On Monday I taught my Tenderfoots how to recognize and treat shock and how to identify venomous spiders. After lunch I served slushies at the Trading Post. On Wednesday Becky sang "Right Field," and later that night I went to vespers. I was starting to think about my life outside of camp. I was about to begin my senior year at Southeast High School. College was on the horizon—I was considering the Naval Academy as a stepping stone to the FBI. (I wanted to be Fox Mulder.)

I remember that last Friday night very well. When dinner was finished, Lucas and Ben stood on the stage of the dining hall and led us in the Seven Ranges alma mater. And as we sang, the summer of 1995 replayed in my mind: the sweet discoveries of that first week, of meeting Trey and Norman, Becky Einhorn, the smell of the path that leads to Handicraft, the way the sun reflected off Lake Donahey during vespers, Lucas's speech about a real Utopia, and my realization that it never lasts.

I was crying and it was the kind of cry that cannot be hidden. My eyes leaked faster than I could wipe the wet away. Lucas, onstage, saw me. He tilted his head and put his hand on his heart and smiled, but never stopped singing.

After Retreat I said goodbye to Eddie Rambler. I wasn't sure when I'd see him again, if ever. Then I followed Norman and Trey to Admin, and instead of crossing into the woods, we walked west along the shoulder of the road for a quarter mile. In the distance I heard the beating of low percussion and I wondered if the men who dressed as Indians liked to sit around a drum circle before leading the ceremonies. But then a horse and buggy appeared over a rise and we realized with amusement that the buggy was equipped with subwoofers thumping bass. A young Mennonite was perched on the wagon, reins in hand. He nodded as he passed, a smile at his lips, as our fillings vibrated to the Smashing Pumpkins.

To the right we found a dirt drive that led to a rusted oil derrick. Until that moment I thought that was all that was back there. That's the point.

"Here we go," said Norman, continuing on.

Beyond the oil derrick, the narrow driveway continued over a hill, and at the top was a gravel parking lot full of cars and a low wooden building that was similar in shape to the shower houses at Seven Ranges, but much larger. Behind it were two rows of platform tents. Older men walked in and out of the building. One of them spotted us and waved us over.

"You're just in time for spaghetti," he said.

"This is James," said Norman. "It's his first time behind the scenes."

"Ah!" the man said, sizing me up. "If you're staying over, there are a couple empty tents."

"Thanks," I said.

He extended his left hand, and when I shook it, he entwined our pinkies in the secret Pipestone way.

"I'm Jim," he said. "Jim Mills. I'm in charge of youth protection for Pipestone."

"Nice to meet you."

"So, who wants some pasta?"

Even though we had already eaten, we were seventeen and always hungry. We walked around the back of the building to a concrete patio. There was a table there with paper plates and plastic silverware and a big metal bowl of spaghetti. A line of middle-aged men snaked behind it. Some were still wearing clothes. A few were completely nude, their beer guts distended above half-hidden peens. The building was, indeed, a large shower house. I could hear the water running now, and the air smelled strongly of Head & Shoulders.

"So," said Trey loudly, "I hear this is where all the dicks hang out."

A couple men laughed. We got some spaghetti and stood off to the side as the elders sat on plastic chairs in a semicircle on the lawn. Only one man, a skinny fellow with a half-engorged member, placed a towel down before sitting.

After dinner the naked men went to the patio, where they began to smear red paint on their pale bodies. No man can successfully paint his own back, so the men would ask their friends to help them. One man I recognized as a local scoutmaster looked to Trey.

"No thanks," said Trey. "I just washed my hands."

Among their ranks were the elders of the Pipestone program. These men wore special black wigs and feathered headdresses. Painted on their chests were the symbols of the ceremonies: Man, Fire, Tee-pee, Flower, Arrowhead. They held a certain status among this elite group. They were first to be dressed.

Soon night came and mosquitos buzzed around us and bounced off the halogen lights of the shower house. Bug spray was passed around. Then, around ten o'clock, a group of painted men walked away, across a long field and into the woods, along a path that led behind the ceremonial circles.

Trey and I followed, but Norman opted out. "I'll see you in the morning," he said.

We kept our distance from the others and eventually the Pipestone elders forgot we were there at all. We followed them through the woods, but stopped short of the ceremonial clearing, where they were preparing a fire.

"This way," said Trey, turning down another footpath. I walked behind him and we soon came to a small, rectangular patch of packed earth, where we could sit and watch the ceremony out of sight from everyone else. I sat beside Trey and we waited for the festivities to begin.

The minutes dragged on, an hour or more. As we waited, the men of Pipestone built the fire high, using those bundles of clean wood the candidates had brought to camp.

"They're coming," someone said.

The Indians took their places, standing below the cow skulls. The chief sat on his stump behind the fire.

We heard them before we saw them—a rhythmic thunder approaching through the old woods, the sound of a hundred feet running along a trail. And then . . . the hiss of the flare sticks. Angry orange light flitting between the trees. The Indians led a group of teenage boys into the clearing and positioned them in rows, like an army of frightened toy soldiers.

The ceremony began, the first boy stepping forward to begin the trials. At some point I came to realize it was the fourth-year ceremony.

After the last boy went through, the chief rose from his stump.

Just then, Trey turned to me. He leaned in to kiss me. But at the last moment, he brought his hand up to block his mouth. It was his go-to joke, but nobody was here to see it. And he didn't move around mockingly or pull away. And after a second I embraced him. I held him and he let himself be held. And in that moment I was at peace.

"Masturbation leads to curiosity," the chief of Pipestone proclaimed.

Trey pulled away, smiling. I sat back, trying to control my breath. My heart hammered in my chest. My ears were ringing. And I smiled, too.

Morning came early with the sound of truck doors closing and cars driving away.

I had spent the night in an empty tent, wrapped in my sleeping bag on a rusty metal-spring bed, after returning from the woods around 2 a.m. I stepped outside into the day and saw some of the Pipestone elders heading to their cars, sleepy-eyed and groggy. They were normal middle-aged men again, teachers and accountants and farmers. You'd never suspect they were in charge of a secret society that taught boys about masturbation and warned them of the dangers of homosexuality, though you might notice some patches of red skin paint around their necks on Saturday morning.

Jim Mills waited behind the shower house, drinking coffee from a Styrofoam cup. He saw me and crossed the yard. "Are you part of my sweat lodge gang?" he asked.

"Yeah," I said.

"Great. But look, don't mention it to anyone else. There's no room for more and I don't want to disappoint anybody."

"Okay."

"Good. We'll get started in half an hour." He walked away with his coffee to join the other adults. I found Norman and Trey and we wandered around the big field behind the shower house while we waited for Mills. Finally the last of the other grown-ups left and Mills waved us over to a camper van that remained on the lot. It was smallish, as far as RVs go, slightly larger than a normal van. He opened the side door and walked into a kitchen/living area with a half-circle couch facing a television set. Another boy was already waiting inside. He was also a staff member, but not someone I knew well. It was Tommy's tentmate, Andrew Lund.

"Take a seat," Mills said as he climbed behind the wheel.

As soon as Trey, Norman, and I were seated, Mills started the engine and drove over the bluegrass field toward what looked like a mound of canvas tarps beside the tree line. As we got closer, I could see that it was a sort of igloo, big enough for maybe six adults. An opening up top let out a steady pillar of smoke.

Mills parked the RV beside the structure and we all climbed out of the back.

"Hang your towels on the back door," he instructed. Then he undressed in front of us until he was completely nude. He knelt down beside the structure, pulled back a canvas flap, and crawled inside the sweat lodge. We looked at each other for a moment. Everything about this seemed off.

"Do we have to get completely naked?" I asked.

"Jim says it's tradition to be fully nude," Norman explained. "But you can keep your underwear on, I'm sure."

But the others dropped trou and so I did, too. I was the last to crawl in. I entered through the sweat lodge door and the flap closed behind me. It was near pitch-black inside. A heap of red coal embers smoldered in the center and provided enough light to see the others after my eyes adjusted. We were seated in a circle, about a foot apart from each other. I sat on the dirt ground across from Mills. It was hot inside, and the air was fusty.

Mills dipped a ladle into a bucket of water and sprinkled some of it over the coals. There was a loud hissing and popping, and the small space quickly filled with black smoke. Andrew coughed loudly.

"It'll clear in a minute," Mills grumbled. "Don't worry."

It was longer than a minute, but the smoke eventually dissipated. It left behind a scrim of soot on skin. We were getting filthy.

We sat in silence, and every few minutes Mills poured some more water on the coals, filling the place up with more smoke, blackening our skin.

"Hundreds of years ago, probably right around here, the local Indians would smoke their peace pipes and then come into a sweat lodge and meditate about their ancestors," Mills said. "The heat and the smoke would cause them to have visions. It's a very sacred space. I recommend you close your eyes and clear your mind and allow yourself to experience the thoughts that come to you."

I closed my eyes and tried to clear my mind. I listened to the sizzle of the coals, the heavy exhalations of my friends. Flashes of images from the summer flickered over the aperture of my consciousness: Trey pounding on the barrel drum that first night of camp; racing through the dark in Lucas's car, while a kid struggled to breathe; the way Mike Klingler had caressed my ear the night he hurt Tommy; the clouds that rolled over themselves above the dining hall the night of the storm; the sound of the cannons alerting everyone to the lost swimmer.

I knew in that moment that one day I would write about these things. I was here to witness these tragedies. I felt a connection to time, an inkling of the years to come, a glimpse at that endless, flat circle.

I felt the summer ending. I knew that when I left this sweat lodge, I would walk to Admin and my father would pick me up. He'd take me back home; back to the real world, where young men steal toys when nobody is looking; back into a house filled with such anxiety that sometimes I fantasized about walking out the front door and turning east and never stopping. Even after all the terrible things, I wished I could live at camp forever. Eden is a dream in the Land of Nod.

When I opened my eyes again, I found Mills staring at my body. He caught me watching and quickly looked away.

When the last of the coals had been extinguished, we crawled outside again and laughed when we saw how dirty we'd become. We were covered in soot from head to toes.

"Don't touch your towels yet," said Mills. "You'll want to wash off first."

I figured we would return to the shower house, which was in sight across the field, but Mills brought out a gravity shower from his RV. He stepped onto the back of the vehicle, between the open doors, and held the water pouch in the air, naked still, his shriveled penis swaying side to side. "I better go last," he said. "Who's first?"

I stepped forward. I was eager to dress again. Norman, Trey, and Andrew stepped around the side of the RV to give me some privacy. I wondered why Mills didn't simply hang the bag on one of the doors. But by then, I kind of knew. I felt the wrongness of this encounter. For a while the fact that Mills was in charge of youth protection for Pipestone had provided reasonable doubt. He wouldn't be given such a role if he was questionable in any way, right? But it was clear to me now that this man simply wanted to see some teen boys naked. I think by then we'd all wised up to it.

In order to get under the shower, I had to stand beside the open doors, which brought my eyes level to his prick. It bobbed up a little as I approached. I didn't waste time. I scrubbed the soot off with my hands, face first and then my body.

We were out of earshot from the others, so maybe that's why Mills was emboldened enough to say what he did. "You have a beautiful cock," he whispered. "But I prefer you with clothes on."

I dried off and grabbed my clothes and jumped into the RV to get dressed. I took a seat on the semicircle couch facing the TV as Trey stepped up to the shower. I noticed there were several unlabeled

VHS tapes on the counter, beside a VCR connected to the television and my stomach dropped. Maybe it was my intuition finally catching up, but I had a vision of Mills setting up a camera in the woods, just out of sight, pointed toward the back of the RV. This man had planned everything so well—telling us to keep quiet because there was no more room, so we didn't say anything to the other adults before they left; the soot providing a reason to shower—all of it. I was so naïve, even after everything that had happened that summer.

Trey came in and dressed and then Norman. Then Mills shouted, "God damn!" and I turned in time to see Andrew step under the shower. His penis was the largest member I'd ever seen. Seven inches flaccid. And thick.

I looked at Norman and Trey and saw the same thing in their eyes. *What the hell did we get ourselves into?*

When Andrew was done, Mills asked him to not get dressed yet and to hold the shower so that he could clean himself. "You wouldn't want to get your clothes wet," he said. Mills took his time. When it was over, they came in and dressed, and then Mills drove us back to the ISH.

"The sweat lodge is a secret," he told us before we left. "Just like Pipestone. It stays with us, okay?"

I walked back to camp with Norman and Trey. Andrew stayed behind with Mills. I have no idea how he got home.

"I think he was getting off on that," I said at last.

"No shit," said Trey.

"It was definitely the weirdest thing I've ever done," said Norman. "I think I need another shower."

My father was waiting in his pickup truck when I returned. I said my goodbyes to Norman and Trey. I embraced them each, but something had changed. We were still processing the sweat lodge and what it implied about Mills and Pipestone itself. And everything was weird now.

I got into the truck and my dad pulled away and drove us home.

now

I got together with Eddie Rambler at South Point one night. I wanted to interview him about Seven Ranges and what he remembered from 1995. He pulled up on an electric scooter five minutes late. It folded up and he leaned it against the wall. We sat on the patio so he could keep an eye on it. To Eddie's dismay, South Point had stopped serving cider, so he settled for a G&T. We talked about our daughters for a bit. Then talk turned to the book and what I'd discovered.

"I knew Jim Mills, too," he said.

"You did?"

"I think it was the summer after you were there, '96, '97? Yeah, he took me to a nudist camp."

"Uh . . . what?"

"He invited me to spend a weekend with him at this nudist camp outside Latrobe, Pennsylvania," Eddie explained. "I was horny as hell and went so I could play volleyball and see some titties, you know? He brought this boy with him, who looked about seventeen. Said he was mentoring inner-city youth or something."

It was beginning to appear that Jim Mills targeted every one of the friends I met at Seven Ranges, at one time or another, and somehow evaded justice for decades.

Jim Mills's luck finally ran out in September 2012, when three boys told police in Gahanna, Ohio, that Mills was giving them pot in exchange for playing "naked games" with them inside his house. He was arrested and charged with pandering sexually oriented materials to a minor. Then, a few weeks later, the Department of Homeland

Security issued a warrant for his arrest on federal child pornography charges. Mills had been videotaping his victims for years. He faced a minimum of fifteen years in prison, at the age of seventy-one. He knew he was caught and he knew he would die inside a concrete cell. So the day he was scheduled to appear in federal court, in March 2013, he placed the barrel of his gun under his chin and blew his brains out the top of his head. A friend found his body in the backyard. Because he took his own life, many details of his crimes were never reported.

When I requested the police reports, I had to explain that I might be one of the boys on his videotapes. A detective assured me that all evidence had been destroyed after Mills's death, but was kind enough to forward me every report they had on the man. There were several and they painted a detailed picture of the last year of Jim Mills's life and how everything unraveled.

On the evening of May 25, 2012, Jim Mills called the police department with an odd complaint. He said he was out of town, but had learned that a teenage boy was throwing a party at his house, without his permission. Was this a grandson or something? they asked. No. It was just some nineteen-year-old boy named Britton who was staying at his home. Mills said that Britton had permission to be there, but was told not to have any friends over.

So a couple police officers drove over to Mills's house and found Britton inside, along with eight others, ranging in age from sixteen to twenty-five. The officers told them to leave and they did.

Then, on June 11, Mills went to the police station to report a stolen credit card. He told them that a fifteen-year-old boy named Jacob did "work" for him sometimes, and earlier that day Jacob was on a computer and Mills was looking over his shoulder when Jacob logged onto Facebook. A friend of Jacob's, who went by the nickname Rico Suave, had posted a photo in which he was holding a Huntington Bank credit card, like the one Mills had recently lost. He called the bank and discovered that someone had used the card to make purchases at the local Speedway and McDonald's. The police learned that Rico's real named was Andre and he was nineteen years old. Mills told the officer that Andre had been in his house the night before with some friends, but he'd kicked them out around 7:30 p.m. He believed that was when the young man stole his credit card.

If the officers were growing suspicious about the number of teen boys coming in and out of Jim Mills's house, they didn't say so in their reports, but it surely raised some red flags.

On August 13, Gahanna police officer Michael Shippitka spotted a car heading east on Route 62, with a cracked windshield and a very loud exhaust. He activated his lights and the car pulled off the road, but as it did, he saw the passenger duck as if to put something under his seat. Officer Shippitka walked up to the vehicle and found four people inside. The driver identified himself as nineteen-year-old Anthony J, who claimed to be homeless and said he was living out of the vehicle. He knew the car needed work, but he had no money to cover repairs.

Officer Shippitka then spoke to the passenger, who turned out to be Britton, the teenager who'd thrown the party at Jim Mills's house when Mills was out of town. The officer was about to let them go, when Anthony, unprompted, told him he could check the car if he wanted.

So that he could perform a search, Officer Shippitka had Anthony, Britton, and the young couple in the back exit the car. Under the carpet on the passenger side, the officer found three credit cards belonging to Jim Mills. And in the glove compartment, he discovered a brand-new iPod.

By then, other officers had arrived. Officer Shippitka told the gang to get back in the car and wait while they contacted Mills. When he didn't answer his phone, one of the officers drove out to his house. Mills came to the door. When they explained what was going on, Mills told them he'd noticed that his cards were gone and was going to report them stolen in the morning. The bank told him there were $2,700 in fraudulent charges currently on his account. Mills was pissed. He told the police he wanted to press charges.

At that point Officer Shippitka arrested Anthony and Britton for receiving stolen property. At the station the officer came to suspect that Britton was high, due to his strangely slow responses. Britton admitted that he'd taken Xanax that day. Both young men were then transported to Franklin County Jail.

It was Anthony who finally told the police what Jim Mills was doing with the boys in his house.

On September 26, Anthony called Gahanna police from the Extend-a-Suites hotel, where he was staying with two teen boys who had been reported missing: fifteen-year-old T.H. and fourteen-year-old J.T. An officer drove out to speak with them in person.

T.H. told the officer that he'd run away from home a couple weeks ago and had since been staying with Jim Mills. "He kept asking me to play strip poker," the boy said. "He asked me to watch the Ohio State football game with him, naked." Mills gave the boy red wine to get him drunk, he said, and then asked him to play naked games again. This time T.H. obliged. Mills brought him to a bedroom and had him lay back on the bed. He asked the boy to masturbate while he watched. While he was doing so, the boy noticed a camera in the corner of the room. Its red light was on, recording.

Anthony told the officer that Mills would give him money if he got naked for him. He said Mills had cameras all throughout his house—in the computer room, the bedroom, the kitchen, and his garage. There was a combination lock on one bedroom door. And he'd recently barricaded his exterior doors with two-by-fours. Anthony warned them that Mills kept a semiautomatic handgun on his nightstand.

Then Anthony provided the police with a video he'd taken on his cell phone, which had recorded a conversation between Britton and Jim Mills in which Mills talked about these naked games.

The police figured it was time they paid Jim Mills a visit. A SWAT team descended on Mills's home. They executed a search warrant and arrested Mills for Pandering Sexually Oriented Matter Involving a Minor. Inside, they found Britton and a seventeen-year-old boy. The teen told police that Mills had asked him to masturbate for him and to put ringlike objects on Mills's penis.

When he was brought to the station, Mills waived his Miranda rights and opted to speak to detectives so he could explain his side of the story. He told them that he was a nudist and that he found the human body to be beautiful. He admitted that he'd gotten three to five juveniles naked inside his house and said there were videos of one of them on his DVR system. He said he only wanted to "spread the wealth about nudism."

Police confiscated videotapes, cameras, and computers from Mills's house. During the search they also found a Polaroid photo of a naked boy that had been taken on a boat. They found it in a desk, next to a picture of Mills completely nude.

Mills had a friend bail him out of jail and returned home. But the police returned on September 29, after a neighbor reported there were still children coming in and out. When police arrived this time, they found a teenage girl living out of a camper on his property. They escorted her home.

The Feds got Mills in November. He was arrested again, this time for "knowingly persuading or coercing a minor to engage in sexually explicit conduct for the purpose of producing pornography that has traveled across interstate or national boundaries." Later that night police arrested a young man named Cory at Mills's residence as he was leaving with Mills's handgun. Cory was charged with Carrying a Concealed Weapon, Drug Paraphernalia, and Possession of Marijuana.

By December, Mills was out of jail again, confined to his house to await trial.

On the day he was due in court, the Ides of March 2013, a man named Matthew Roubanes called Gahanna police to report that Jim Mills was dead. The circumstances of his death are as odd as Mike Klingler's.

Roubanes told police that he had arrived at Jim Mills's house at 8:52 a.m. to pick him up for his court appearance. He was an old friend of Mills's, another Scout who had gravitated toward him when he was a teenager. Roubanes said he had found Mills lying outside his house, naked, with a suicide note left beside the body and a revolver by his feet. The suicide note was not handwritten, but had been typed and printed out. The cause of death was a gunshot wound to the head.

I attempted to contact Roubanes to learn more, but he did not return messages left on his voicemail.

I did, however, track down his ex-wife, Barbara Roubanes-Luke.

"Jim Mills was a groomsman at our wedding," she told me. "They were very close, ever since he was a boy." Roubanes helped Mills put together a child-safety program for Pipestone, she explained. "That was one of their projects—this new system where no one adult would ever be alone with a minor, that way nobody could be falsely accused of doing the wrong thing."

Another project of theirs, she said, was the system of cameras that Roubanes helped Mills install inside his home.

"I think it was around 1994," she said. "I remember Matt was at Mills's home two or three nights a week. He told me he was fishing wires through the walls. It was an expensive project. He told me that it was a security system, but I never understood why they were doing it. When I heard about what happened with Mills, everything I thought I knew about him went out the window."

She believes her ex-husband knows more about the circumstances of Mills's death than he's ever told police. It was no accident that he was the one to discover the body, she said.

"Matt told me that he provided Mills the gun that was found next to the body," she said. That, she believes, makes Mills's death, at the very least, an assisted suicide. Mills had no intention of going to prison.

As for the young boys who lived with Mills near the end, the transient teens he housed in exchange for playing naked games, I have tried my best to track them down and have come up empty-handed. I visited many a desolate and desperate apartment complex on the outskirts of Columbus—the sort of places where the weight of depression seems to make the walls lean in—hoping to speak with Britton or his friends. But they never stay in one place very long and their phone numbers change too quickly for me to discover through records.

I was playing a hunch. But every instinct told me I was on the right path. The question I wanted answered more than anything else, the question that could explain so much about the summer of 1995, was this: Did Jim Mills abuse Mike Klingler, too?

then

I started my senior year of high school two weeks after camp closed.

I reunited with old friends in the hallways and I listened to their stories about trips to amusement parks and Virginia Beach and summer jobs at Taco Bell. And when they asked what I'd done, I simply told them I had worked at a summer camp. "It was fun," I said. "Lots of free slushies."

There was a disconnect with my peers that had never been there before. They had lived through their summer. I had survived mine.

At night I lay awake, thinking about how circumstance is the roadwork of fate. If that boy hadn't have breathed in that poison ivy smoke, I would not have had the leverage to ask for the room at Admin. I would have stayed in CIT-ville. Would I have been the one Mike Klingler favored? Would my tent have been the one he slipped into at night? He did love my ears.

I had other concerns that fall. My stepmother's verbal abuse ramped up exponentially upon my return. Perhaps she felt the need to make up for lost time. I stayed away from home as much as I could. I found a new hobby—amateur filmmaking. I had never asked for anything of value from my father. Money had always been tight, especially when he worked at the steel mill. But he was running a construction business then, and we could breathe, so I asked him to buy me a camcorder so I could make movies with my friends. Most evenings that fall I rode around town with my buddies Bill, Blake, and Travis, shooting scenes for a *Die Hard* rip-off that I edited using two VCRs wired together. When we were done, we rented out the town hall and

I quit Boy Scouts. Every time I thought
about putting the uniform back on,
I was consumed with anxiety.

a popcorn machine and charged $5 admission for the premiere. We made $200.

I quit Boy Scouts. I told my scoutmaster I was too busy. I was two merit badges and a service project away from making Eagle. But every time I thought about putting the uniform back on, I was consumed with anxiety.

Instead, I tried out for the fall play, *Rehearsal for Murder,* a closed-room mystery about an actress who appeared to commit suicide, but really she was killed. I played one of the suspects. The little sister of a boy from my Scout troop played another supporting character. Her name was Julie.

Julie was third-generation Hungarian, with a cute, round face and hazel eyes. She was the only one backstage who didn't laugh at my jokes. She only rolled her eyes. I saw it as a challenge, I think, to make her laugh. It was never easy.

"You should take her to Homecoming," her brother told me one day.

But the thought of attending a formal dance terrified me. And besides, it was the same week as the premiere of my movie.

When it came time for dress rehearsals, Julie would apply my makeup and the paint that gave me white hair around my temples so I could play an older man. We'd sit on chairs facing each other in the green room and I'd look at her as she did my eyelashes—so close I could feel her exhalations against my skin. She'd catch me staring and she'd smile knowingly. That's what the beginning of our relationship was, a lot of her catching me noticing her, spotting her spotting me in the hallways as we walked to class, sneaking a peek down her low-cut costume dress as she leaned toward me to deliver her line. I felt the quiet magnetism of it.

After the play I got her number and one night I called her at home.

"I was hoping you'd call," she said.

I asked her to go to Pizza Hut with me. She said yes.

I finally had the inspiration I needed to get my driver's license.

The day of our date, I passed the maneuverability test. I was almost eighteen.

I drove her to Pizza Hut and I paid. I was making $60 a week showing homes for my dad's business, all cash under the table. ("Here's the spacious half bath with subway tile walls.") That night Julie laughed at one of my jokes. I don't even remember what I said.

After dinner we ended up at her friend's house—the girl's parents were out of town. We sat together on a big recliner and watched a horror movie in the dark, and halfway through I kissed her. After weeks of foreplay our hands were suddenly all over each other. We made out for hours, until my cheeks were numb and her lips were puffy.

The next weekend I drove her to a donut shop in Kent, in my car, a '79 Monte Carlo I'd gotten from a distant relative. It had bench seats, and on the way home, Julie slipped out of her seat belt and cuddled up to me. I put my right arm around her, driving not so well with my left hand. She wore a white angora sweater and it felt delightful under my fingers.

We became inseparable overnight. I drove her to school and back. Her house was across town from mine, so I'd get up early and drive past the school, out to her house so that we could talk all the way back. At the end of the day, I'd drive her home. We had an hour before her mother arrived after work and so we'd run upstairs to her room and take off our clothes and stay under the covers for as long as we could, until I got back into the Monte Carlo and drove around the block until her mom came home and then I would return.

"I love you," I told her that Christmas.

"Thank you," she replied.

When school started again after the holidays, the drama department decided to present a series of one-act plays. I got to direct an adaptation of Edgar Allan Poe's "The Raven." I had to lead rehearsals three nights a week. It may have been the first bit of creative responsibility I'd ever been given, and I took it very seriously.

One afternoon the Monte Carlo refused to start. Usually, I could spray ether into her carburetor and she'd come alive again for a day, but not this time. Linda was home and had no plans for that evening, so I asked if I could take the family van.

"No," she said.

I explained my responsibility to the drama team.

"No," she said again.

So I swiped the keys and took it, anyway.

I was halfway through rehearsal when my father showed up. His face was a mix of rage and fear. He pulled me aside and explained that Linda had called the police and reported the van stolen. "You have to come home with me right now and straighten this out," he said.

I left then. I had no choice. He drove the van back and I rode shotgun. I felt some resolve inside me break at that moment and I lashed out at my father. All the terrible things I'd thought to say to him over the years came flying out of my mouth. "How could you fight so hard to get custody of me and then leave me with her?" I yelled.

By the time we pulled into the driveway, I'd said unforgivable things. Whatever these years had been building toward, I understood that it was happening now.

He parked and then lunged at me across the seat as I lunged at him. I got off one punch and it connected with his left eye.

At that moment the police arrived. One cruiser. Two officers.

"Fuck!" my dad said, his hand over his eye.

We got out of the van. My dad was blinking away the pain, but his eye was watering as a bruise quickly formed there.

"It's all right, we've got the van. There's no issue here," he said.

But the police were not stupid.

"What happened to your eye?" one of the cops asked.

"Nothing. Nothing happened."

"Did you hit him, son?" the other cop asked.

"You bet I did," I said.

They arrested me on the spot. They handcuffed me and put me in the back of their car. I remember my father breaking. I remember him crying. And I remember Linda watching from the window.

I was taken to the juvenile detention center in Ravenna, a large concrete building behind a barbed-wire fence beside the adult jail. They had me undress in a room with a window, where a jailer watched me spread my cheeks. He reminded me of Jim Mills. Then I put on a pair of prison scrubs and socks and they walked me to a cell I shared with another teenage boy who'd stolen a car and had gotten caught.

"How long will I be here?" I asked.

The judge would decide in the morning, they explained.

I wondered what Julie would think when I didn't show up to pick her up at 7 a.m. Would she be mad?

My bed was a concrete slab with a firm mattress on top. They gave me a scratchy blanket, too. It was getting late by then, so I just lay there, staring at the ceiling, wondering if my cellmate would rape me, like they joked about in movies sometimes. I started to cry.

"Shh," said a kind voice.

A boy was sitting at the end of my bed. Apparently, there were three of us in the cell. I must not have seen him when I came in, because I was so absorbed in my own pain.

"I'm Mike," he said. "What happened to you?"

"I hit my old man," I said.

"Why?"

"Because his wife hit me."

"Sucks. But why are you so upset?"

"I'm scared."

"It's not like the movies," he said, as if reading my mind. "It's safe here. The guards are cool. Most of them. They look out for us. Food's not bad. I don't mind it here. You're going to be okay. You should sleep."

"I don't know if I can."

"That's Russ, over there. He's already asleep. Nobody's going to mess with you."

"Okay."

"You'll be fine. Promise."

Five minutes later, I was asleep. They woke us up at six o'clock the next morning. Daylight shone through a barred window, illuminating the small room with its two beds. Mike was not there.

A judge released me that morning, back into the care of my father and Linda. I returned to school and explained to the drama director what had happened. She asked if I wanted to continue with the play. I did.

I found Julie at lunch. I was afraid she'd look down on me for hitting my dad, but she didn't. When we were alone again, she put an arm around me and held me while I cried.

After that, I started eating dinner with Julie's family every night. They let me stay until it was time for bed. Her dad ran an auto body shop in Ravenna, where he played classical music on the shop stereo while he worked on cars. Her mother was a teacher. Being there could be overwhelming sometimes, the affection they showed to each other and all of their children.

The fallout from my arrest made home awkward, everyone too afraid to say anything that would stoke the vile animosity again. I apologized to my dad. He got a real shiner, which lasted for two weeks; and every time I looked at him, my body went chill with shame.

At the end of the school year, the senior class took a trip to Cedar Point, this large amusement park on Lake Erie, with some of the world's tallest roller coasters. I took Julie and we walked through the park, hand in hand. I got to third base on an indoor coaster that was part haunted house, part space station. On the way home we shared secrets. I won't tell you hers. I told Julie about my experience with the boy at camp when I was eleven. I told her a little about the last summer, about how a man had tricked me into getting naked with some other teen boys, about how a man had died and we didn't know why.

For graduation that year each student got four admission tickets to give out to family members. My dad and Linda got theirs. My mom another. But my mother was single at the time, which meant I had one left over, so I invited Lucas Taylor.

On the day of the ceremony, my mother arrived at school with a bundle of sage and took me into the cafeteria, where there were plenty of open windows and some privacy. She lit the sage on fire with a gas station lighter. I thought for a moment that she wanted me to smoke it.

"It's called smudging," she said. "It banishes negative energy." She moved the smoldering bundle around my cap and gown and blew some smoke in my face. It smelled quite pleasant.

When she was done, I walked her to the gymnasium, where the graduation was held that year, and introduced her to Lucas.

"How you doin', bud?" he asked.

I started to reply, but my voice broke with emotion. He hugged me. He made a graduation card appear in his hand. "For later," he said. I tucked it in my back pocket.

Julie was standing with the choir and I waved at her as I joined my classmates. I had no idea what I was going to do next, but I no longer wanted to be an FBI agent. I wanted to stay near her. I wanted to marry her. I wanted to have a family with her.

I got all that. And a little more.

now

Everything led back to Jim Mills. His secret proclivities aligned with
Mike Klingler's and I suspected a connection between the two. It
was no more than a hunch, a feeling. I had no proof Mills even knew
Klingler. Not until I tracked down Ian Shore.

Ian was the Ecology director at Seven Ranges the summer of '95,
Lauren's boss. I remember his blond Afro and how he took charge the
night of the storm. He was one of a few counselors I reached out to
who actually replied. We spoke over the phone, because he lives on
the West Coast now.

"I have a lot of fond memories of camp," he said. "It's where I fell
in love with nature. I loved the nature walks, teaching Scouts how to
identify edible and medicinal plants. I teach middle school biology
and science now. And I love it. I'm not sure that would be my life if
not for Seven Ranges."

Ian quit Scouting after that summer, though. The tornado spooked
him. He understood how close we'd come to losing Scouts that night.

"It was too late to fire the cannons," he recalled. "So I ran up the
trail behind the dining hall to warn the troops back there. But the
storm got there first. When I came off the trail, there were platforms
flying around in the air. Tents everywhere. That was traumatic enough,
but it came so soon after Klingler. It did something to me. Changed
something about how I looked at camp."

"Do you remember a guy named Jim Mills?" I asked.

Ian sighed loudly. "I knew Mills very well. He was a mentor of
mine for many years. I worked closely with him. Did you know that he
was in charge of youth protection for Pipestone? I can still remember

how he told us that child molesters target victims without a strong father. That those boys are easy targets. He was literally telling us how he operated. In retrospect, it's just stunning. But why was I never victimized? I wonder about that a lot."

And so I asked the question: "Did Jim Mills know Mike Klingler?"

"Mills knew Klingler very well," he said. "They were very close."

"And the arson," I said. "The Trading Post. Do you think—"

"It was Klingler? Yes. There was a fire at my house, too, around the same time. And Klingler was there when it happened. Luckily, nobody was hurt. But I know that before he died, Mills talked to Klingler about it. He pleaded with Klingler to stop torching shit."

There it was. The answers I'd been searching for since I was seventeen. I felt goose bumps raise over my arms.

"Why do you think he was starting fires?" I asked.

"He was crazy," Ian said. "We really had no idea about the demons living inside Klingler. But he must have been very troubled."

After Mills was accused of sexually assaulting children, Ian texted him to check in, as he did periodically over the years.

I find myself in some trouble. I'm not prepared to talk right now, Mills answered.

That was the last time Ian ever heard from him.

"I don't really know why he was nice to me and a terror to other boys," Ian said. "But I think about it a lot."

I found Andrew Lund, Tommy's tentmate, in a rehabilitation facility on the outskirts of Canton, recovering from a second stroke, even though he's still in his forties. He was standing outside when I arrived, leaning on a metal walker. I helped him fold it up and put it into the back of my Subaru and then we went to a local restaurant to talk.

In the summer of 1995, Andrew showed up to camp and expected to run Waterfront. He'd worked there the year before and enjoyed the job. But Scooter made him camp commissioner, instead. His job was walking the camp after breakfast to inspect the cleanliness of each site. A Scout is clean, after all. At the end of the day, the troop with the cleanest campsite was awarded a "coup feather" at Retreat. He hated the job. Didn't want the responsibility. It also essentially exiled him from the rest of the staff. It was a loner job. He officially shared a tent with Tommy, but also kept another tent across camp, behind Watersports, which is where he spent the majority of nights.

"I could always tell which troops had money and which troops did not," he said, recalling the job. "The system was unfair in that regard. Because the wealthier troops had nicer things and the means to keep it tight. So if the poor troops tried hard, I'd give them the feather, even if their site wasn't quite as clean as the rich kids'."

Andrew first met Mike Klingler inside Jim Mills's sweat lodge one weekend after Pipestone in 1994. But he was formally introduced to Klingler during setup week the summer I joined staff. Everyone knew that if you wanted to score smokes, you could get them from Andrew. So he figured Klingler wanted cigarettes when he came to his tent one night. "But the next thing I knew, we were wrestling on the floor and he was trying to get my clothes off." Andrew sighed and shook his head. "Mike was a strange bird. I think he was closeted. When you were having sex, he was into it, but when it was over, he'd call you a faggot. He would get very violent afterward, like it was your fault he was gay. You knew what you were getting with Mike. But Mills . . . you never knew where you stood. You never knew what was going to happen next. You could see the turmoil in Klingler's eyes. There was nothing but evil inside Jim Mills."

Mills would often drive to Andrew's house and pick him up for the day. He even met Andrew's parents. And by the summer of 1995, he was using the kid as often as he could. "Mills was the first one to come into my tent," he said. "He couldn't control himself. You knew he was going to take it, one way or another, and I wasn't a fighter." He was too embarrassed about what was happening to tell his parents.

Later, when Andrew heard that Klingler had died, he only felt relief. "I had one less problem to worry about."

Mills continued to abuse Andrew for months after Klingler died, until the pig roast at Camp Tuscazoar that fall. Years ago, Tuscazoar was the premiere summer camp for boys in the area, but after Seven Ranges opened, it was mainly used by local troops for off-season events. That fall Andrew's troop held a pig roast there. Each family brought a potluck side of some kind (beans, mac 'n' cheese, etc.). While parents prepared the meal, Mills walked Andrew to his camper van, which was parked far away from the festivities. Andrew thought he was relatively safe because another man, a friend of Mills's, was walking with them.

But once Andrew was inside the van, Mills closed the doors and the other man stayed outside. Mills told Andrew to remain still while he tied him up. By then, Andrew knew the routine—Mills had already introduced him to BDSM. And his misadventures always began with some kind of restraint. He removed the boy's pants. That's when Andrew saw the other man watching through a window. He suddenly understood that he was in a lot of danger. This was by far the most brazen attack Mills had ever attempted.

"There were adults everywhere," said Andrew. "But he couldn't help himself." Maybe that's why Andrew decided to finally fight back. Maybe he'd just had enough. But this time Andrew grabbed Mills by the throat and squeezed. Mills tried to pry him off, but Andrew was young and strong, and Mills was old and chubby. Mills began pounding on the side of the van, but his friend took off. He didn't want any part in what was happening now. At the last moment Andrew let go and Mills fell to the floor, gasping for breath. Andrew threw open the door and jumped out, half naked, a rope trailing from his wrist. He ran to the grown-ups, and when they saw him, everyone went quiet.

"It's Jim Mills," he shouted. "He's fucking crazy." Then he ran into the woods, where he hid until his mother came for him and dressed him and helped him walk back.

Shortly after this event Buckeye Council placed Jim Mills on its ineligible volunteer list, but I can find no record that they ever alerted the police. Anyway, Mills was never charged in that incident. And Andrew did not know who the other man was that day.

The events of that summer replay continually in his mind, like a record where the groove is scratched, causing the needle to skip. Alcohol and drugs provide momentary relief.

"These monsters from '95 are there all the fucking time," he said, pointing to his brain.

For many years Andrew has been on a long journey to recovery from PTSD, from the nightmares that place him back in that sadist's van. He's in a better space, psychologically, now. But years of self-medicating have taken their toll. His liver is shot—he's been sent to hospice twice and he suspects he has some cognitive decline. "I've pickled my brain," he said.

In 2013, Andrew slipped in the shower and hit his head on the way down, resulting in a traumatic brain injury. He has suffered from seizures ever since and it probably contributed to the two strokes he's had. This latest one happened while he was at work—he inspects steel pipe for stress fractures at a factory not far from his house.

"Everything happens for a reason," said Andrew. "But I'd love to know the reason for all this."

—————————

Forgive me. I didn't believe him.

Even after all I had learned about Jim Mills and Mike Klingler, it was hard for me to believe that Mills could have attacked Andrew at such a public event and gotten away with it. How could so many adults turn a blind eye? Was it possible Andrew was exaggerating the story for some kind of gain, a possible monetary reward from the victims' trust fund?

It was a difficult story to verify. Mills was dead and I had no idea who else was at the pig roast, or if I could find them after all these years. I could only think of one other person I might talk to—his mother.

I drove to her house in the country, outside Alliance, one summer day. Beverly Lund lives in a cottage house surrounded by immaculate flower beds full of a variety of colorful perennials. I found her out back, near a decorative pond full of shubunkin goldfish and pigmy lilies. It is a contemplative space, very zen.

"I know you," she said, after I introduced myself. "I read your story about Pipestone." She invited me around to the front stoop, where we could sit on a couple soft chairs and look out at the hills.

She and Andrew were estranged, she explained. The last time she'd spoken to him was Christmas. He had a girlfriend she didn't approve of, or who didn't approve of her.

"I tried to reach you at the newspaper, after the article came out, but I think you'd already left. I wanted to tell you what I knew."

It was true, she said. All of it.

"Jim used to come to our house and pick up Andrew and take him on little trips. We didn't question it, because everyone knew who he was and had the greatest things to say about him. He'd come right up to our door. Look at our faces. Then he would take Andrew and do terrible things to him. I was home that day. I got a call from Camp Tuscazoar. They told me that Andrew had said Mills did something to him and then ran into the woods. Nobody could find him. So me and his father drove down there."

When they got there, Andrew's father walked around the camp, shouting for Jim Mills. They found him in the parking lot. She thought her husband might kill the man. But Mills denied he did anything inappropriate. He said Andrew was trying to ruin his reputation.

It took an hour to find the boy. He was deep in the woods, hiding. His mother walked him back to the car and they drove home.

"He told us not to call the police," she said. "He was so embar-rassed about that whole thing." Instead, she spoke to Jack Johnson, the Buckeye Council executive, and Mills was no longer able to attend Pipestone or to visit Seven Ranges, but he stayed active in Boy Scouts and even attended local Eagle ceremonies.

She said Andrew ripped up his Eagle certificate when they got home. "It broke him," she said. "Whatever happened in that camper, it broke him. We were a close family before all this. But after that day everything changed."

Before I left, Beverly asked me for Andrew's new phone number. They spoke later that day and made plans to get together. I felt a little better about my intrusion and lack of faith, knowing it had led to a reconciliation, however brief it may prove to be.

I found Lauren on Instagram. She is unrecognizable, though I imagine I am as well, with my thinning gray hair and extra weight around the middle. Lauren is thin, athletic, and tatted—there's a red, naked demon lady along one arm. She divides her time between an apartment in Pittsburgh and Canton, where her daughter lives with Lauren's ex. She relies on friends to get her back and forth because she does not currently have a valid driver's license. I drove to Canton to take her to lunch one day. It was the first time we'd seen each other since 1995.

The first thing I noticed when she invited me into her daughter's home was the turtle she kept in an aquarium. It was set up in a glass tank, like the ones at Ecology, where she worked at Seven Ranges. The years at camp were formative for us in so many ways, and the things we do today are echoes of that time. She still surrounds herself with creatures of all kinds.

Lauren completed all five years of Pipestone before she left the Boy Scouts (unlike many of us, she returned to work on staff in 1996). But she eventually became disillusioned with it, too. She placed her stone inside Ranger Bob's casket when he died a few years ago. Ranger Bob was a quiet old man who mowed the grass at camp and dispensed life advice periodically. Her Pipestone token went back into the earth, like the sacred pipes of the Lakota.

I told her about the old friends of ours I'd tracked down. As far as I've discovered, we can be divided into two categories—those who could never escape the past, and those who did. I guess I'm somewhere in between. "That was also one of the best summers of my life," she said. "I'm proud of myself for seeing it through. It was my first job and I was good at it."

Eventually we got around to Klingler.

"I took his death very hard," she said. "He was always kind to me. I lived in the rooms above the dining hall and he'd come up at night and we'd drink coffee and talk. He was there almost every night. He brought me old staff shirts to wear."

The day Klingler was escorted out of camp, the day he died, Lauren had gone home. She doesn't remember why—just that she had the night off. When she came to camp the next morning, she couldn't find anyone. She didn't know that we'd been called to the dining hall so that Scooter could tell us about Klingler. She knew something was wrong, but went to Ecology to set up for her early merit badge class. Then a Scout came in and asked her if she knew who the staff member was who'd "blown his lid."

"I didn't know what he meant. But then another counselor came in and walked straight to the back office in Ecology without saying a word. I followed him back there, where we had some privacy, and he told me what Klingler did. I lost it. I started screaming, crying. It was awful. Some scoutmaster came in and took over my classes for that day. I just remember saying, 'It's not possible, it's not possible.' And then I went to find you. But you were already gone."

"Wait, what?" I said.

"You left camp and you didn't come back for a while. Days."

I told you, my memory around that event is wonky. Jumbled images and remembrances. But I definitely don't remember leaving. If anyone could confirm that, it would be my father.

On my way home I called my dad.

"Hey," I said. "Back in 1995, did I come home early after Mike Klingler died?"

"Yeah," he said. "You called me. I remember it was late at night, like around eleven. You called me at home and said I might see something on the news about camp, that your friend had been assaulted and another counselor was dead. I asked you if you wanted me to come out that night and get you, but you said no, that it could wait until morning. So I came early the next day and brought you back. You stayed for a few days, just processing, I think. Then you asked to go back."

"I don't remember."

"You were really upset."

"Can you come out here?" I asked. "Can we get a drink or something? I need to tell you some things."

"Sure," he said. "How about tomorrow? We can shoot some pool while we talk."

then

I went to college so that I could teach English. If I wasn't going to join the FBI, I thought I'd enjoy teaching kids how to write. I enrolled at Kent State and got a dorm room in Dunbar Hall, across the field from where the students were murdered by the National Guard in 1970. I got a single room that measured sixteen feet by five, little more than a closet. Big enough for a bed and a TV. But it was mine. For the first time ever, I had a place of my own. Julie was there all the time, man. And it was fantastic.

I got a job at a movie theater. Started as an usher and worked my way up to projectionist. This was before the digital wave, so every Thursday I spliced together reels of 35mm film onto wide platters for the Friday premieres. Everything from *Twister* to *Titanic*. The only machine I can service, to this day, is a Christie projector. I still can't drive a manual car, but I can take apart a projector and put it back together again. The benefits of working at a movie theater were killer for a college student on a tight budget—I could take Julie to any movie for free, with a small popcorn on the side. And when my car wasn't working, I could walk to work.

Our student newspaper was called the *Kent Stater*. You could find it in newspaper boxes all across campus and in town, too. And it was free. At the bus stop everyone had a copy. Everyone read the paper back then. If you had a cell phone at all, it was still just a phone—it didn't have the Internet. You relied on the paper for your gossip, your scuttlebutt. I wanted in on that. And so I began to submit opinion pieces. By my sophomore year I had my own weekly piece: "James and the Giant Column." The editors let me write about anything I wanted, so long as it related in some way to campus life. I wrote columns making fun of the university's president, the cafeteria food, the football team. But my most popular pieces were about a local towing company that preyed upon the student body.

City Towing had contracts with the larger apartment complexes near campus. If you decided to drop by to visit a friend, but didn't have a permit, one of their trucks would swoop in and snatch your car as soon as you were out of sight. The drivers worked in tandem with spotters on the ground, armed with walkie-talkies, who would wait for someone without a permit to park illegally and then call it in. It was a well-organized racket, and if you were a student at Kent State in the late '90s, you almost certainly had your vehicle towed by these guys at least once.

I went after them relentlessly. For shits and giggles I would stand outside the apartment complexes and wait for their spotters to arrive and then I would alert everyone by shouting through a megaphone: "The British are coming! The British are coming!"

Eventually management caught on to my vendetta and responded in kind. They cut out my photo from my *Kent Stater* column and turned it into a Wanted poster, which they hung in their office: *Reward for the first driver to tow Renner's car.* I shit you not.

I knew they were after me, so I was very careful about where I parked. For years I watched my back. For years I avoided their gang. But then, the week I graduated, I had a final in the Michael Schwartz Building and I was running late. There was a visitors' lot at an apartment complex across the street, and since half the student population had already gone home for Christmas break, the spaces were empty. I took a chance. My final took all of ten minutes, and when I was done, I ran back to the lot to discover that my car had been towed.

Naturally, I was pissed. Now, what I should have done was show up at their office with a box of donuts and congratulated them on their win. But since I was twenty-two, and thought the world owed me, I took a bus that dropped me off around the corner from their business and walked over to their lot, where I found their gate wide open, my car sitting right inside. I had the keys in my pocket. And I made the calculations about how quickly I could run to my car, start it, and drive away. The math checked out. I figured the company was so shady, they wouldn't even call the police. I figured possession was nine-tenths of the law. I figured a lot of stupid things. And then I ran to my car.

It's apparent at forty-five, looking back on twenty-two, that this was an orchestrated trap. As soon as I entered the gate, three men came running out of the shop. I managed to unlock and enter the car before they got to me. I locked the doors and put the key in the ignition. But like some terrible horror movie, my car refused to start. And that gave them time to catch up to me.

One man pounded his fist on the driver's-side window. A second man stood at the passenger side and began to use a slim jim to try to unlock the door. The third, a man I later came to learn was named Jeff, stood in front, blocking my way, holding a comically large wrench. "Get out of the fuckin' car!" he shouted. "Boy, I'm gonna fuck you up!"

Just then, the car started. I nudged it forward and Jeff climbed onto the hood. He dropped the wrench and grabbed hold of my windshield wipers. "Now, what the fuck are you gonna do?"

I floored it.

There is some debate about how far I drove with Jeff on my hood. He would later tell the police that I drove with him on the hood for at least four hundred feet. I think it was more like forty. But in any event I slowed down after a moment and let him off. He tried to punch through the driver's-side window, but it didn't break. And I rode off into the sunset.

I made it as far as the university before I got pulled over.

A cruiser caught me, lights spinning. I pulled over to the shoulder in front of the new rec center and waited while the officer came up to my window. Now, I graduated in December. That's an important detail for how things worked out. It had snowed that morning and everything was covered in a dusting of white powder, including my

Sunfire. I rolled down the window and, as calmly as I could, I said, "Morning, Officer."

"Morning," he said. "Mind telling me where you're coming from?"

"Oh, I had a final. Just finished up. I'm on my way home."

"That the story you're sticking with?"

"Yeah."

"Could you step out of the car, please?"

I got out and the officer walked me around to the front of the car and pointed at the hood. Like I said, the car was covered in snow. Except, that is, for the perfect outline of a man stretched out over the hood, like some character from a Road Runner cartoon that had smashed into the side of a canyon wall. "Mind explaining this?"

I hung my head. "I did something really stupid," I said.

"Yes, you did. Turn around."

I did what he said. He cuffed me and put me in the back of his cruiser. My car was towed again, this time to the city impound. I was taken to the police station, where I was charged with vehicular assault, a felony. In short order I was arraigned at the local courthouse and then transferred to the county jail, where I was placed in a holding cell until someone could bail me out. I used my call to contact Julie's father, who worked nearby. But it took him a few hours to make the arrangements.

While I waited, I sat quietly in a holding cell, which was only slightly larger than my old dorm room, and contemplated my future. At the end of the week, I would have my degree, but what job could I possibly get with a felony on my record? All that hard work over the last four years had been for nothing. I saw years of washing dishes at restaurants in my future. I'd probably have to work for my dad, hauling cinder block for basements, being paid under the table. I felt sick. I was a blob of shame and self-hate. I'd thrown up my breakfast at the police station. My stomach was empty. And my head swam with nausea. If I could only have a little something to eat, maybe I'd feel better.

The door to my cell opened and a young man stepped inside

carrying a Styrofoam lunchbox. He wore an orange jumpsuit, like an inmate.

"You hungry?" he asked.

"I am," I said.

He sat on the concrete ledge that served as a bed/couch and handed me the container and some plastic utensils. I opened it up to find an assortment of chicken nuggets and fries and corn. Starch and starch, but I didn't complain.

"Thank you," I said.

"It's James, right? James Renner?"

And that's when I realized I knew this young man. It was the boy from juvie, the boy who'd comforted me that night. "Oh, my God," I said. "You're Mike."

"We gotta stop meeting like this," he said with a smile.

He stayed with me while I ate, told me that he'd ended up there after getting into a fight outside a bar in Ravenna. By the time I finished eating, I was feeling better. I sensed a glimmer of hope, even. I had stopped feeling sorry for myself, anyway. At least briefly.

"You'll be out soon," he said. "You'll be fine."

"Thank you," I said again.

Mike took the empty container and stepped to the door. A buzzer sounded and then he exited.

And maybe about now, you're wondering if Mike was real. I've been wondering the same thing. I think about it sometimes, how unlikely it is that I saw the same boy both times I was in jail. And both times he comforted me when I needed it most.

I wouldn't see him again for twenty-two years. And even now, after meeting him a third time, I'm not sure.

––––––––––

I didn't go to prison. The day of the trial, the prosecutor reduced the charge to a fifth-degree felony (attempted vehicular assault) and the judge sentenced me to probation, community service, and counseling. I worked off my community service at a food bank, where I packaged meals into Styrofoam containers and delivered them to the homes of the elderly or infirm. I liked the comradery of the volunteers, the acceptance of everyone because everyone was struggling—we were working there either because we were in trouble or because we needed a free meal. And it was good to have someone to talk to—the anger management counseling sessions were often deep dives into my relationship with my stepmother. I was not yet ready to admit that I had been abused, but I was beginning to understand how I had learned that violence was an acceptable response to a disagreement.

I had recently gotten a job at a new movie theater in Hudson and I stayed there instead of applying for better jobs. I wasn't sure how the felony thing would play. If I stayed out of trouble for three years, I could get it expunged, though. So I kept my head down and did my work in the meantime.

I had a graduation party. The mood was somber, given the situation. It was held at the community hall at the trailer park where my father and Linda were living. He'd lost the business and the house after some bad deals and that's where they ended up for a bit. Linda gave me my favorite gift that day: a leather satchel, the kind real reporters owned. I still have it to this day. But here's the thing: It was so out of character that I understood right away what it was. It was the last thing she'd ever do for me. Sure enough, she divorced my father a couple months later. I met my dad at a McDonald's, where he told me how he'd been served with the paperwork. My response was simply: "I'm so happy for you."

"I'm done with women," he said. "I'm never getting married again."

now

My dad married a kind woman named Darla on July 7, 2007. That's 7/7/07, which he thought was a lucky day and a good omen. She was the daughter of a preacher from Detroit and she came with three children of her own. In fact, it was that preacher that took in my sister, Jo, when she had some trouble as a young adult and fixed her up and sent her back whole again. If you believe in fate, my dad eventually learned that he and Darla had first met as children, at a random campground, when their families had set up tents next to each other one day, round about 1965. Sometimes things work out. It just takes time.

I met up with my old man at Victory Lanes in Springfield one evening. He's a very different man now, from the man who raised me. I was his first family. For a while his only family. Now he has six kids and nine grandchildren. He's quieter, gentler. He has a long gray beard. Last year he sliced his right hand in half-feeding a plank into a blade on a construction site. The doctors sewed him back together, but some of the fingers on that side don't move so well anymore.

Victory Lanes is mainly a bowling alley, but there's also a room with a bar and a few pool tables near the back. That's where we met up. My dad brought his own cues in a long case. He used to hustle. We had a red felt table in the stone-floor basement when I was growing up.

"Two Miller Lites," I said to the bartender as my dad took the stool next to me. She poured our drinks and then busied herself at the other end.

"So, what's up?" he asked.

"I want to tell you about some things, but I want you to promise me you won't kill anybody."

"Okay."

And so I told him what happened with Craig when I was eleven. He listened quietly, but his eyes started to leak a little at the sides.

"I thought maybe you already knew," I said. "I asked you to take me to a counselor once, when I was sixteen. I needed to get it out, I needed to tell someone. That's what I told him. I figured he told you everything."

My dad shook his head. "No. He wouldn't tell me what you said to him. But he did call me. I remember I was showing a home that day and he called me at work. He asked me if he thought you would tell him the truth."

"What did you say?"

"I told him that yes, what you told him would be the truth. But I said you would also tell him what he wanted to hear. So he should make sure not to let you know what he wanted to hear first."

I've thought about that statement a lot since then. I'm still picking it apart. It sounds true, though.

"What else?" my dad asked.

I was forty-five years old, but it was still hard to say the thing I always wanted him to know. "I was in love with a boy that summer I worked at camp," I said. "I liked girls, mostly, but I liked some boys, too. I really did. I had friends over the years that I fell in love with, but I could never tell them how I felt because I was afraid of how you would react. I wish I had been able to tell them how I felt back then."

He sighed and nodded. He looked at the bar.

"Why were you so afraid of me being gay?" I asked.

He brought his hands up to the bar, his right one hooked a bit. He brought his palms together and then divided them by a few inches, like brackets, against the counter. "I have to live in here," he said. Then he moved his hands apart several more inches. "So that you can live out here."

Oh, the feels. Of all the goddamn, misunderstood things. All this time he had viewed it as a sacrifice. I love this complicated man.

"We can all live out here, Dad," I said.

"I don't think so, bud," he said. "I think if we did, everything would fall apart."

I want to think he's wrong.

We drank our beers and we talked about less serious things, and after some time we played pool. And even with his gnarled fingers, he had to let me win.

––––––––––

My mother got her nursing license a few years ago. She works at a sober treatment facility on the west side these days, running group therapy sessions for addicts of all kinds. Lately she's been visiting a sweat lodge, where sober people can meditate. It sits in a field out in the country and is run by one of her old, hippy friends.

I took her to lunch one day so that I could tell her everything I'd told my dad.

"I wouldn't have cared if you were gay," she said when I was done. "I just didn't want you to be a nerd. I used to pick you up on the weekends and you'd be wearing dress shirts with the collar buttoned."

She reached out and took my hands. "But I wish you had felt like you could have told me what happened to you back then. I wish you had felt like you could have come to me."

I wish I had, too. My mother understands trauma. Over the years she's shared some of it. At lunch that day she shared some more. Her parents were poor. Her father disappeared when she was little and she was told he died in a car accident. That wasn't true, but she wouldn't know any different for many years. In fact, he was very abusive and was essentially run out of town by the family. After that, she and her mother and her three sisters went to live on her grandparents' farm. There my mother was repeatedly abused by one of her uncles. He'd sneak into her room at night when everyone else was asleep. When she was twelve, she took a bottle of pills. "I just wanted to make it all stop," she said. When she didn't die, she was sent to the psych ward at

Akron General (the very same hospital where I would be committed later). When she got out, she was placed in foster care, where she remained for a couple years. She met my dad in high school, got pregnant with me at eighteen.

Drugs and alcohol provided moments of peace for a tumultuous mind. But eventually it only compounded her problems. "If there was a way to be high forever without it destroying my life, I would," she explained. "Who would want to live with all of this trauma? Nobody. But that's not living, either."

AA has been successful for her. She doesn't drink. She doesn't take narcotics under any circumstances. And I've never seen her cheat, not even when she was in excruciating pain before her knee surgeries. But there are still bad days. She disappears still, sometimes for days. But it happens less and less.

I suppose you don't have to be Freud to recognize why I made a career out of searching for missing women. I've been doing it since I was three, ever since my mom disappeared in the night.

———————

I finally confessed to Trey. I chickened out and did it in an Instagram DM. I wrote many versions of the message and deleted them, again and again, before I settled on a final draft. I didn't want to say something like, "I'm sorry if this is uncomfortable," or "I'm sorry if this is weird." I didn't want to apologize for feelings I had thirty years ago that were totally appropriate feelings to have. Here's what I settled on:

> *Hey man. So I'm getting deep into this book. I met up with Lauren and it was helpful to remember some stuff. There's one awkward bit I've been kicking around, even though it's 2023 and it shouldn't be awkward. I had a crush on you, in '95, in the way I'd have a crush on a girl at school. But I was terrified to ever voice that for fear of embarrassment and because I valued our friendship and didn't want anything to harm that. And I'd like the freedom to say so in this book. Is that ok?*

I waited anxiously for Trey to reply from Sweden. And when he did, it was in classic Trey fashion. Just two words: *For sure.* He followed up five minutes later with, *I might suggest clarifying some of these details with those closest to you.*

I replied: *I've always been honest with Julie. I think that's why we've lasted so long.*

then

The day my mind broke started like any other.

I got Casey and Laine off to school. Made my breakfast and coffee. Read the Drudge Report. Wrote a few pages of a novel. I noticed a creeping anxiety on the periphery of my consciousness, but that was to be expected. I had stopped taking my medication the week prior. I had gained too much weight and I blamed the meds instead of the booze and pot munchies. I thought that by not taking them, I could lose a few pounds. I knew there would be some withdrawal symptoms, that I might feel some of that old anxiety and depression again, but I felt mentally healthy and I thought I could power through it. Obviously, on some level, I was aware that I was being irresponsible, because I didn't share my plans with Dr. Deb or my psychiatrist.

A part of my routine was different that day and this random deviation probably saved me. The air-conditioning unit in my Subaru needed to be charged, so I met Julie at the mechanic's shop after she was done teaching for the day and I got into her car and we went to pick up Laine together. Any other day I would have been alone.

Laine is in middle school and the way student pickup works is you pull into a one-way drive that leads to a parking lot in front of the school, with an exit on the other side. You find a parking space, get out, collect your kid, and then walk them back to the car.

Julie was driving. She turned into the entrance to find that a large truck was blocking the way to the parking lot. It had stopped in the middle of the lane. So she put her hazards on and got out to find Laine in the gaggle of fifth graders waiting by the door.

I got out and walked to the truck. A man sat behind the wheel, reading something on his cell phone. His windows were open.

"Excuse me," I said. "You can't park here."

"What's that?" he said in a low voice.

"We have to keep the lane open. Fire hazard. And the other parents can't get through."

"Okay, boss."

"Thanks."

I started back toward the car. I saw Julie coming with Laine. But then I looked back at the truck. The man had not moved. And now he was standing outside, leaning against the hood.

"Motherfucker," I said. I walked back toward him.

Now, this man was easily 250 pounds and not fat. Looked like he knew his way around a bench press. I am, to put it kindly, unathletic.

"You gotta move your truck, man," I said. "It's not safe."

He stood straight and said, "Maybe you should make me."

That's all it took. That was the crack in the dam. There is a rage monster that lives inside me, something I keep locked away so that my kids never see it. It was born in those knock-down, drag-out fights with Linda. I knew how to be cruel. I was taught by a master.

"We can absolutely do that," I said to the man, crossing the distance. I felt a joy then, in the sloughing off all civility and pretense. I wanted to hurt this man. I understood that he would overpower me. But I needed to feel my fists on his skin first. I needed him to feel that pain, the embarrassment of being at the center of a scene he thought would not happen.

"James Renner!"

It was Julie. She saw me and she read the situation in the way only a spouse possibly could.

"James Renner, get in the car!"

I looked back at her. And then I turned back to him.

"Don't!" she screamed.

If I had been alone that day, I would have fought that man. I would have lost. I would have lost so much. And I likely would have ended up in jail again.

It took every ounce of strength I had to walk back to the car, instead. I got in and Julie pulled through the crowd and took us out the back way.

My mind was still infected by that rage and there was nothing, no medicine, no happy serotonin, to dampen it. "I can't believe you," I said to Julie. "I can't believe you did that. You made me look like an asshole in front of all those other parents."

"You were going to get yourself killed!"

I yelled at her, and at some point I realized Laine was crying in the back seat. She was ten and she'd never seen me yell at her mom. This was not a man she knew. I had worked so hard to be someone better and I was ruining it.

"You're too old to do stuff like that anymore," Julie said. "You can't. I need you. I can't have you going to jail."

She drove me home and then left to take Laine to get shoes for softball practice. I slammed the car door as I got out and didn't look back as they pulled away.

I had broken some contract with my daughter. I felt it fully. She now had that image of me in her head forever, the rageful man who said mean things to her mother—my best friend, the one who'd stayed with me through it all. And without the meds I could feel the full darkness of my shame, unfiltered. And then I remembered the bottle of pills I'd kept when I quit. Just in case I ever needed them again. I had over a hundred Citalopram. I figured that was probably enough to get the job done. On the heels of that thought came another: You are not totally in control of yourself. And that was a frightening realization.

I didn't go inside. It seemed to me that if I allowed myself to be totally alone, behind closed doors in this moment, I would finally do what I've long imagined. And I was surprised to discover that there was a part of me that didn't want to die. In fact, there was something deep inside me that rebelled against the idea. And that gave me hope.

I sat in my driveway and ordered an Uber. It arrived five minutes later. I got in the back seat and the driver took me to Akron General, without a word. We were halfway there when my father started calling my cell. That meant Julie had been concerned enough to call him. And that meant he knew, to an extent, what I was thinking. He's always been able to read my mind. I didn't have the strength to talk to him, so I sent it to voicemail, over and over, and I'm sure that worried him, and I feel awful about that, too.

I texted Julie: I'm checking myself into the psych ward at Akron General. I'm sorry for how I acted. I guess I really did need those meds.

Then I turned off my phone.

The hospital was not far. When I entered, they sent me to a triage waiting room that was halfway full already. I took a seat beside a young woman who was passing time by scrolling through apps on her phone. "It's a long wait," she said. "They brought me in for assessment three hours ago and I haven't been called back yet."

I nodded. I was pretty sure they wouldn't be sending me back to the waiting room after they evaluated me.

"Renner?"

A young nurse was standing by an open door. I went to her and she led me inside a small room with a chair. I sat down and another nurse cuffed my arm to take my vitals.

"What brings you in today?"

"I'm either going to kill myself or I'm going to kill someone else," I said. "I don't feel that I'm entirely in control of my actions right now."

"His BP is 185 over 120."

"You need to calm down before you have a stroke," someone said.

"I can't." I was crying by that time. Admitting that I was not in control, saying it out loud, had opened up a well inside me and the emotion was rushing out.

"Get him to Psych," someone said.

Two nurses walked me through a back door, down a hall, and

into another unit. I entered a room where the only thing inside was a bed. No computers, no supplies. Just a bed facing a window. I was asked to undress and place all my clothes and belongings into an oversized plastic bag and to put on a blue gown and orange socks with soles that gripped the linoleum. Once I was dressed, the nurses took my stuff and left. I don't know if the door locked behind them, but I'd put money on it. I lay on the bed and waited.

A few minutes passed before a short, older woman came in. She stood beside me. Her eyes were kind, but she had a steeliness the younger nurses lacked. She understood what I was capable of. She'd seen it before.

"What was your plan?" she asked.

"Pills. I have a bottle with a hundred or so Citalopram."

"Are you currently taking the medication?"

"No. I went off them a few weeks ago. I didn't tell my doctor."

"That probably wasn't smart."

I smiled. "No, in hindsight it was probably a really stupid thing to do."

"Your blood pressure is too high. We need to give you something for that soon. Now, I'm going to give you a choice. You can sign this form and commit yourself, in which case you can go home in a couple days. Or I can pink-slip you and you'll be in here for a while longer. What'll it be?"

"I'll sign," I said.

"Good choice." She handed me a pen and I signed her papers. "I know it doesn't feel like it right now, Mr. Renner, but it's going to be okay. You did the right thing. Sit tight while I figure out what to do with you."

I lay back on the bed and tried to busy my mind with counting the grooves in the ceiling tiles. It conjured memories of middle school, the times I would go to the nurse's station when I was feeling overly anxious. I didn't know they were panic attacks back then. But there were times when I'd become so restless, I couldn't concentrate and I'd ask to go to the nurse. She'd let me lie on a bed in a back room until I calmed down. Counting the grooves in the drop-ceiling tiles always helped.

Another nurse appeared at the door. "Your father is here," she said. "Do you want me to bring him back?"

I shook my head. "I don't want anyone to see me like this."

She nodded and disappeared. I half-expected him to push through security and come back, anyway, but, thankfully, he didn't.

About an hour passed before I was taken upstairs. The Psych Ward at Akron General is divided into two units separated by a long walkway. One side is for violent offenders, the other is for harmless "crazy" people. They took me to the violent wing and I'm serious when I say this, they told me it was only because they didn't have room in the other wing. And I admit that could have been a white lie.

They put me in a room with another man, who was quite younger. He lay on the bed and never said a word to me the entire time I was there. They gave me a Trazodone and I lay on the other bed and concentrated on slowing my breathing. Eventually I dozed, but I didn't sleep. My mind was a rush of disjointed anxieties. I wondered if by committing myself I'd crossed some threshold from which there was no return. This is how it started with the writers I admire most: David Foster Wallace, Spalding Gray. I met Spalding once, not long before he stepped off the Staten Island ferry. It was at a writers' workshop in Cleveland. He complimented my scarf.

They called everyone to the common room for dinner. They served us trays of food from a cart, piecemeal hospital items in individually wrapped plastic—juice and Jell-O and such. Sad little salads with one tomato. The diners were a mix of women and men. As far as I could tell, there were two personality types represented—the manic and the zombies. I sat beside a man who wouldn't stop talking.

"I asked for coffee with dinner!" he shouted at the cart server.

"You can't have coffee," the orderly answered.

"Dr. Miller said I can have coffee."

"Take it up with Dr. Miller."

"Fuck you, man." He turned to me. "I don't know why I can't

have coffee. I can have all the drugs I want in here, you know? But they always forget my coffee."

"That sucks," I said.

"Yeah, it does. Shit. Here, did you get one of these?" He handed me a sheet of paper with a list of food items. "It's breakfast. Put your name on top and then give it to that asshole with the cart. They'll bring you what you want in the morning."

"Thanks."

"What did you do to get in here? You beat someone up?"

"I signed myself in," I said.

"Lucky. They pink-slipped me. I'm here until Dr. Shu says I can leave."

I nodded.

"It ain't that bad, though, right? They let us keep our doors open during the day. You can come out here and talk to other people. Food could be worse. Better than I get at home. I always gain like ten pounds when I'm here. Mostly everyone is cool. Stay away from Alvin, big guy in the corner. He's not right in the head."

"Okay."

"What's your deal, though?"

"They say I'm depressed."

"Fuck, man, everybody's depressed. State of the world. Welcome to it!"

After dinner I went back to my room. Every few hours someone came by to check my vitals. My blood pressure was down by then, now that the Trazodone was working. They gave me Citalopram and Buspirone, too. Eventually I fell asleep.

The next day Dr. Shu came to our wing and I met with him and his assistant inside a conference room off the common area. The doctor was around thirty-five, unsmiling.

"I'm feeling better now," I said, which was at least partially true. "I think it was just going off the meds. I'm back on them. I'd like to go home."

"I don't think that's a good idea," he said. "I think you need to stay with us for a while. I spoke to your wife. We talked about your drinking. If you keep drinking as much as you are, you will die. And probably fairly soon. Is that what you want?"

"I just don't want to feel sad anymore."

"You realize alcohol is a depressant, yes?"

"Yes."

"And you're also doing drugs?"

"Well, pot."

"How often?"

"Every day."

"You said you might kill someone or yourself."

"I was angry. I'm not angry anymore."

"You and your wife have kids."

"Yes. Two."

"Maybe consider this as a time-out, then. You did the right thing by coming here. I don't want to release you, just to have you come right back in."

"How long?"

"I'll talk to Julie again. Let's revisit all this tomorrow, see how you feel. You're here tonight, okay?"

"Okay. Any chance I can be moved to the other wing?"

"We're short on beds at the moment. But I'll ask."

I went back to my room. The other guy had gone home and for the moment I had it to myself. I didn't know that this was where my mother stayed when she was twelve. Looking back on it, I wonder if it's possible we stayed in the same room? How long ago would that have been? 1970. 2022. So, fifty-two years. Time is a flat circle.

And now we come to it.

It was late, of that much I'm sure. The door to my room opened and a man dressed in a nice uniform entered. He had a round face and thin hair. He wasn't one of the orderlies from the unit. Everything about him suggested administration. He was familiar, but I couldn't place it.

"James, you're moving to the other unit in about ten minutes, how does that sound?"

"Sounds great," I said.

"Good. How have they been treating you in here?"

"Fine."

"And how do you feel?"

"I feel better."

"Are you a danger to yourself?"

"No."

"We all need a little time-out sometimes."

And then I asked the oldest question in existence. "Do we know each other?"

He smiled. "I get that a lot," he said. "I suppose it's possible. Most people remember me from jail."

The man pointed to the badge on his breast: MIKE.

When you're awestruck, it can feel like terror. I understood the implications right away. This was impossible. There was no way I could be seeing this man right now. The man who'd comforted me as a boy in juvenile detention, the man who'd brought me food in lockup when I was a young man.

He saw all this and smiled openly back at me, waiting.

I understood something else, that if this really were true, if this was really happening, it was against the rules to acknowledge it out loud. I was afraid of what might happen if I did.

"What would you like, James?" he asked.

"What do you mean?"

"Ask me anything. If you could have anything right now, what would it be?"

I was scared to ask for anything important. What were the rules? What were the consequences of asking for too much?

"I'd like Starbucks. A tall Pike Place, please."

"How do you take it?"

"Splash of milk, one Splenda."

"I can do that."

Mike walked out of the room and returned less than five minutes later with a tall Starbucks coffee, still steaming.

"They'll come to walk you over to the other unit soon," he said. "You won't see me again. I do hope you feel better."

"Thank you," I said.

When he left, I sat on my bed and sipped the coffee and considered what had just transpired. I've thought about it for a year now. I will give you a few possible explanations:

1. *Mike never existed.* I have to accept that as a real possibility, given that I've only seen this man in times of heightened stress—and once in a mental institution. My chart reads: *Depression without psychotic features.* But maybe that's not entirely accurate.

2. *The Third Man Factor.* This is a legit thing that happens sometimes, and for which we have no real explanation. People in high-stress situations have long reported the presence of a man who has appeared beside them, to offer comfort. When Sir Ernest Shackleton and his men became stranded in Antarctica during an expedition, he took two other men with him on a long hike to seek help. During that journey he claimed he often counted four among their party, instead of three. He believed something else had joined them, pushing them onward over the mountains and glaciers. Survivors of shipwrecks have reported similar extra people. One theory about the Third Man Factor is that it is a primitive coping mechanism of our bicameral minds, a projection of a piece of our own consciousness, lending needed support. A sort of hologram, which only we can see and hear.

3. *Religious Visitation.* My aunt believes it was either the Archangel Michael or a demon pretending to be him. Am I important enough for divine intervention? The critics say no. And would a demon bring me Starbucks?

4. *It's Mike Klingler.* Is it a coincidence that his name is Mike? If you believe in the afterlife, if you believe in ghosts, could it have been the boy version of Mike I'd never known and the older man he never got to be?

You know what it felt like to me, when Mike was in my room?

Remember Agent Smith from *The Matrix*? He had this ability to take over the body of anyone in the program in order to be closer to his enemy. That's what it felt like. Like an outsider who'd stepped into our silly simulation for a few minutes. A referee, perhaps.

I want to say the coffee, at least, was real. But how can I prove that to you now?

Another nurse arrived a short time later and brought me to the other wing, which resembled a college dormitory and not a prison at all. Their common room had televisions and tables with books and puzzles. I was given my own room and they let me keep some hygiene items there. I could take as many hot showers as I wanted. Still, no shoes with laces, though. There was a cell phone I could sign out from the front desk and I used it to call Julie.

"I'm sorry," I said.

"I'd rather you go to the hospital than jail," she said. "You did the right thing."

"How's Laine?"

"She's good. I told her you gave yourself a time-out because you acted out. She gets it."

"Thank you."

"Why in the world would you go off your meds?"

"I thought they were making me fat."

"There are about a hundred calories in a shot of vodka. I don't think it takes a rocket scientist to figure out where the weight is coming from."

"I hear you."

"I love you, Renner. But sometimes you can be really dumb."

"Thank you."

"Come home."

I called my father next and apologized for dodging him on the way in. "Thanks for trying," I said.

I took the phone back and paced around the wing from my room to the common area and around again. I was surprised by how many older women were there. Women in their seventies, eighties, grandmothers you'd spot at Acme buying bread. I'd never considered that grandmothers could ever be unhappy. But of course. Of course. Somehow that made me feel a little better, but sad at the same time. Sometimes we need this, but we don't talk about it and maybe we should. Because it's very likely you know someone who's spent time in a place like this. We're all struggling.

I slept soundly that night, and in the morning they served coffee at breakfast. Dr. Shu came to see me around lunchtime.

"I think you should stay a few more days," he said. "Sit in on group."

"I'll do better at home," I said.

"I'll talk to your wife, and if she agrees, I'll sign off on it. But if we send you home, are you going to kill yourself?"

"No."

"I believe you," he said. "If you were wondering if you really need your medication, now you know."

"I guess so."

And so I got out after two days. In many ways it felt like my brief visits to jail, only this time I didn't have a trial hanging over my head. My body ached. I desperately wanted a drink. But the misadventure scared me enough that I remained completely sober for several weeks.

I announced my sobriety in a tweet the day I was released. About an hour later, a man named Norman reached out over DM. I hadn't spoken to him in ten years. *Godspeed,* he wrote. *Life is much better when you are sober for it.*

Memories of Seven Ranges flickered across my mind. Maybe it was time to consider how much of what happened to us as kids created these addictions of mine. I wondered if my friends were doing any better.

now

During my reporting for this book, I reached out to the Boy Scouts of America central office several times seeking comment. Calls went unreturned. Emails went unanswered. Then, in March, I received a message from Charles Mead, the director of Marketing and Public Relations: *Hi, James—Appreciate your inquiry. I'm connecting you with Scott Armstrong (copied), our national media lead.*

Armstrong is the president of Advocacy, Inc., a lobbying and communications firm headquartered in Pennsylvania. He was also once the head of the Boy Scouts of America's Longhouse Council. His website is, how should I say . . . strangely low-rent for such an important position. He did not return calls or emails.

But the Boy Scouts taught me to be resourceful and so I enlisted the help of my friend, Mike Lewis, founder of Lewis Investigations, a private detective agency on Cleveland's east side. And that's how I was able to track down Michael B. Surbaugh, the thirteenth chief Scout executive of the Boy Scouts of America, who served as the head of the organization from 2015 to December 29, 2019, which included some of the most turbulent years for the BSA.

When I caught up with Surbaugh, he was at Sea Base, a high-adventure Boy Scout camp located at the end of Lower Matecumbe Key, in Florida. Sea Base provides training in scuba diving, sailing, and fishing for Scouts and is second only to Philmont in popularity among older boys. He and his wife were landscaping around the facilities. Even though Surbaugh no longer runs things, he's still actively involved with Scouting. He's currently working with Sea Base Scouts

During my reporting for this book, I reached out
to the Boy Scouts of America central office several
times seeking comment. Calls went unreturned.

to save the coral reefs off the Florida coast, raising and planting thousands of baby coral along the ocean bottom.

The way Surbaugh tells it, he never intended to lead the Boy Scouts, but kept getting promoted. He started as a Boy Scout in a Pittsburgh troop, joined staff at a summer camp after graduating, and became a canoe guide on the river. He just never really ever left Scouting and eventually the Boy Scout executives came calling. Soon he was working as a Scout executive at councils across the country, including a tenure in Sioux Falls.

"If you pursue your passion and do a good job, people will notice," he said.

By 2015, the Boy Scouts of America was beginning to enact some major changes that would forever alter the traditions of the 105-year-old institution. They had just lifted the ban on gay Scouts, and because of this, there was a lot of tension between the more progressive members of the group and their largest sponsor—the Mormon Church. There was a growing call for girls to enter the program. And meanwhile, more and more former Scouts came forward to file claims against the BSA following the $18.5 million verdict for Kerry Lewis and the release of the perversion files. What they needed was a true Scout to guide the organization through the rough waters churning around them, the sort of man who exemplified the ideals of the program. So, of course, they went to Mike Surbaugh.

His first real test came in 2017, when President Trump addressed more than thirty thousand Boy Scouts at the National Jamboree in West Virginia and went off script to use the opportunity to attack his enemies, a very un-Scout-like thing to do.

"I go to Washington and I see all these politicians and I see the swamp," he said to the Tenderfoots in the crowd, who were there to see the most powerful man in the United States government. "And it's not a good place. In fact, today I said we ought to change it from the word 'swamp' to the word 'cesspool' or, perhaps, to the word 'sewer.' But it's not good. Not good."

He went on to vilify the "fake media" and say, "By the way, just a question, did President Obama ever come to a jamboree?" And, "I saw him at a cocktail party and it was very sad because the hottest people in New York were at this party."

My favorite line, though, is probably this: "As the Scout Law says, 'A Scout is trustworthy, loyal' . . . We could use some more loyalty, I will tell you that."

Soon Surbaugh's phone was blowing up. On the other end news reporters from around the world asking if Trump's speech reflected the feelings of the Boy Scouts of America.

Surbaugh was forced to release a statement: "I want to extend my sincere apologies to those in our Scouting family who were offended by the political rhetoric that was inserted into the jamboree. That was never our intent. . . . For years, people have called upon us to take a position on political issues, and we have steadfastly remained non-partisan and refused to comment on political matters."

Five years later, Surbaugh still cringes when recalling that debacle. "I was watching his speech with my wife at the back of this crowd," he said. "Whenever he went off script, we would look at each other and go, 'Uh-oh.'" After the event he said that the head office received upward of ten thousand letters voicing either displeasure with the remarks Trump made or how Surbaugh tried to walk them back in his statement. It was a no-win.

Then Trump started telling reporters that he'd spoken directly to the head of the Boy Scouts, which would be Surbaugh, and was told that it was "the best speech ever." Except Surbaugh never made that call. "He literally lied," he said. "A Scout has to be honest. I did not make that call."

But what can you do? It's Trump.

Surbaugh's biggest victory for Scouting was opening the doors for girls and women. He wanted to restructure the program so that the whole family could be involved. The council of executives was stubborn and didn't really want to change, but Surbaugh recognized that the change was already happening, with or without their support. "I would show them statistics, sales of our merit badges. We were selling twice as many awards than we had registered Scouts in some of these troops. That's because girls were participating and could not be formally recognized. So they're do everything the boys would do and not be able to receive their Eagle. It was unfair."

After girls were allowed in, the Boy Scouts rebranded to Scouts BSA. Surbaugh says the response on the ground was mostly positive, once scoutmasters saw what the girls could add to the program. "I've heard from dozens of scoutmasters who have reached out to tell me how their program has improved," he said. "There's this collateral effect we never expected. The girls can be very focused in a way that maybe boys aren't. So on campouts the boys see the girls setting up tents better and faster and it pushes them to do better, too. The boys are becoming better Scouts."

And yet, for each positive letter, Surbaugh also received death threats from ultraconservatives who will never accept girls in Scouting. "It was a really difficult time," he said. "But when things would get bad, I would just look at the letters from the young women who were happy to finally be recognized for their efforts."

Eventually I asked him about the abuse scandals and what it was like to be at the epicenter of such a reckoning. I expected him to be cagey and circumspect, but he was candid in his thoughtful response, which amounts to this: Abuse happens in every youth organization, whether it's Scouting BSA, the Boys and Girls Clubs, church groups, or local schools. Whenever you provide a private environment between adults and children, lines will be crossed. Why should the Boy Scouts of America be the only one forced to provide restitution? Where's the big settlement if a kid was abused at the local YMCA? Wouldn't victims be better served if some kind of national trust was set up for all survivors of childhood sexual abuse?

The reason the Boy Scouts of America is on the hook, when others aren't, is because they kept detailed records of the abuse from the very beginning.

"We were the only ones keeping records," he explained. "Some other youth programs allowed boys seeking father figures to be picked up by strangers, single men, who would take them back to their apartment for the day. Meanwhile, the Church would just move their offenders to another diocese. And when something happened and someone sued them, they would say, 'Oh, well, we don't have any records.' No records, no court case."

Surbaugh said that the true purpose of the aptly described perversion files has been misinterpreted. It was never about protecting Scouting or protecting the leaders involved. It was about protecting the children. Before Scout leaders became mandatory reporters, they were already gathering information about potential abusers and sending notices to headquarters so that those men could not simply move to another troop in a different state and start abusing more kids. It was the first national database of sexual offenders. But it was a database full of uncharged suspects. These men had not been convicted of a crime, so there was nothing legally to be done, but there was enough suspicion that nobody felt comfortable putting them around boys. From the point of view of Surbaugh, the Boy Scouts of America went above and beyond to protect their Scouts.

Still, over the years, some men managed to slip through the cracks of the perversion files, men like Timur Dykes, who abused Kerry Lewis and many others after confessing to similar crimes years before.

"It's never going to be risk free," he said. "Nothing is. But what other organization was keeping records and using them to protect children? None of them. We did the right thing and were severely punished for it, while others were not. And eventually the liabilities outgrew the funds for the BSA. The only thing you can do then is file for bankruptcy."

And here's why I like Surbaugh. He stepped up when others were afraid to. "I knew what was going to happen when I took the job," he said. "But I thought I could help to structure the organization so that it could survive through it. Sometimes you do what you're called to do, even if it's going to be difficult."

Where Scouting goes from here, he says, will be up to the families involved. "Scouting has always been a reflection of the values of the parents."

Surbaugh said one more thing before we finished. He said there was no room in Scouting for secret societies.

———————

Last Friday the drums beat for the Pipestone ceremonies at Seven Ranges as they have for nearly one hundred years. When I first wrote about Pipestone in 2005, Buckeye Council executive Jack Johnson promised me that they would remove the talk about masturbation and homosexuality from the program. I learned later that this didn't happen.

When the Boy Scouts of America declared bankruptcy, the head office asked each council to donate money to help pay for the settlement provided to the eighty-two thousand Scouts who were victims of abuse. According to court documents, Buckeye Council contributed $1,945,529 in cash and $669,000 worth of property.

So far, the victims have not received a dime. Some, like Eric Palmer, are waiting to see if their state legislators will adjust the statutes of limitations so that they can be fully compensated when the payout finally happens. Ohio House Bill 35 passed the House, but at the time of this writing, it is still in committee in the Ohio Senate, as insurance lobbyists try desperately to keep it from progressing.

And even after all of this—the scandal, the bankruptcy, the damage done by Jim Mills—Buckeye Council still allows Pipestone to continue because they believe it draws Scouts who would, otherwise, visit other summer camps.

The new executive director of Buckeye Council is a man named Jesse Roper. I asked him why he continues to allow this secret society to operate inside his camp.

"Pipestone is not a secret organization," he said. "Over one hundred thousand Boy Scouts have participated in the program. How could something that big be secret?"

"You're saying it's not a secret organization?"

"That's right."

"Do you think the parents of your Scouts would agree with you if they were to see the ceremonies and hear the speeches given by these chiefs? How do you think they'd respond if they saw everything that happens at the secret shower house that's hidden across the street? And if it's not secret, then why is the password 'secrecy'?"

"You're not recording this, are you?" he asked.

Calls and emails to Boy Scouts HQ went unanswered for months. I attended a convention in Dallas in June and gave myself an extra day to drive to its main office in Irving. The parking lot was nearly empty. The building is nondescript and has a neglected vibe. There's nothing about it that feels like the headquarters of a great organization. When I asked the receptionist if somebody was there I could speak with, I was given a business card for its PR spokesman, Scott Armstrong. He's a lobbyist operating out of Pennsylvania. Calls to his office went unreturned.

Nobody seems to want to be the person to end Pipestone. But it's past time they did. It is the worst sort of cultural appropriation, a pidgin, racist play loosely based on the traditions of the very people whom we stole this land from. If a boy wants to understand the history of Pipestone, let him journey to Minnesota and hear it directly from Travis Erickson.

Boy Scouts, the organization created by Robert Baden-Powell, a closeted homosexual who once killed a god, cannot learn from its mistakes. It is, at its heart, a club that brings boys close to men. And men, inherently, are dangerous beasts.

I contacted Baden-Powell's descendants. He is still much revered by his family. *We are all VERY proud of him,* wrote Robin Clay, Baden-Powell's grandson, in an email to me.

When I asked about the revelations regarding the relationship between Stephe and the Boy in Tim Jeal's biography, Clay said it was all taken out of context:

Jeal had his own agenda. He needed to make his book "sensational" in order to increase sales. He put his own

interpretation on everything and omitted what didn't suit his
purpose. He was allowed extremely rare access to all the stuff
held by the Boy Scouts of America but following that book,
the BSA vowed never to allow another author to see it again.
In the army, men build up very close relationships with fellow
soldiers. Jeal was never in the army so would not be able to
understand that sort of close bond.

When I followed up with questions about Baden-Powell's letters to Scouts about masturbation, I received no further responses.

———————

So what really happened to Mike Klingler in the field behind his house that day?

The investigator for the Stark County medical examiner could not determine if it was murder or suicide. I can see both scenarios playing out. Klingler would have been arrested in short order, probably later that night or the next day. The truth about what he did to Tommy was going to come out, one way or another. He was done teaching. Any cursory investigation by police at Seven Ranges would have included interviews with staff members, and that would have brought them to Andrew Lund, which would have led to further charges against Klingler and then the crimes of Jim Mills would have been revealed. Klingler's death halted any further investigation and allowed Mills to continue his predation.

And while Jim Mills had the most to gain by Klingler's untimely death, and he had access to guns, I think it's unlikely he killed Klingler. It was Klingler's own gun that ended his life. And Janette, next door, saw nobody else in the field, only Klingler's feet flying into the air after the gunshot. I'm confident, now, that Klingler's death was a suicide. He ended his life to avoid the shame of what he had done. And that suggests that there was still enough humanity in him to feel terrible about it.

Mills was beyond salvation. Whatever evil gripped him tight was more powerful than whatever spark of goodness was left in him. It is incredible that he still acted on his impulses after Klingler's death, after he'd barely avoided detection when it all happened. In fact, he continued to prey on Tommy's bunkmate. He truly could not help himself. He'd given up.

Would Klingler have become a predator if not for Mills? Hard to say. But I think not. Mills was his confidant. I think if he'd chosen a good man to confide his sins to, instead of a monster, he could have found the help he needed before he went too far. But we'll never know for sure. By the time I met Klingler, he was already a rapist and an arsonist. He'd already passed the point of no return.

And how far do I care to follow the trail in search of an explanation that satisfies me? Do I look for someone who made Mills the way he was? Was it his scoutmaster, sixty years ago? And what about that man? And the man who made him? I search for a beginning, when it's the endless circle again.

Eventually someone must break the cycle, the way Eric Palmer did. He shared his story instead of keeping it secret out of shame. And sharing the story of abuse led him to seek out the help he needed to live with it, to recover from it. Whereas Dan Burris, who worked closely with Eric's rapist, became an abuser himself and is now serving fourteen years for raping two other Scouts.

For Jim Mills, Pipestone served as an endless buffet of wayward boys. He didn't need to tell them to keep their relationship secret—the Pipestone program had already told them how important secrecy was. The ceremony was something we didn't share with our parents, with anyone who wasn't a member. It was easy for Mills to expand that circle of trust to include his naked games. And it's hard to believe the other adults who ran Pipestone didn't suspect what was going on—everyone could see the sweat lodge at the edge of the property, after all.

Buckeye Council's continued obsession with Pipestone is hard to fathom after all the fallout from the abuse scandal within the Boy Scouts. It is tradition for tradition's sake, without reason or reflection. It only continues to exist because Seven Ranges is located in a remote region of a Midwest state, far from the oversight of the head office or any sizeable jurisdiction of the law. There is no justification for it. I'm confident of this, simply because whenever I explain the program to someone outside of Northeast Ohio, the response I get is universal and identical: "What the actual fuck?"

Remember what I learned the hard way: You don't realize it's abuse if it's the only thing you know. That's why Pipestone starts when you're eleven years old.

The inappropriate interactions I experienced at Seven Ranges maybe don't rise to the level of legal abuse, but they definitely shaped the way I saw the world forever after. I was always an inch from danger. I got lucky. If I'd stayed in CIT-ville with Klingler, maybe I wouldn't have the strength to write this story. He almost killed Tommy. What might have happened if he'd chosen my tent? I hope that this book might change things for the real victims. But I'm not optimistic.

What can you do? If you see something, say something. If you've been abused, tell someone. And then tell the police. You are not alone. You're a part of our brotherhood now. And you don't have to paint your skin red to join our group.

I want to say one last thing about the systemic abuse inside the Boy Scouts of America. Jim Mills did untold damage to a generation of boys at Seven Ranges. But he is only responsible for a single claim in the bankruptcy settlement. There are at least 81,999 others like him.

I've been thinking a lot about my stepmother lately and about all the things I never got to know about her. I was never curious about her life. I never asked her what her life was like. So one day I reached out to an old friend of hers who keeps in contact over Facebook: *I'm writing a new book that is mostly about my experience with the Boy Scouts when I was a kid. But some of it has to do with my relationship with Linda. Would it be ok if I asked you some questions?*

Certainly, she replied.

Here is how our conversation unfolded:

"I don't know much about Linda's childhood. Was it tough?"

"Yes, I believe it was. Are you looking for something specific?"

"Just trying to understand her better. Why was her childhood tough?"

"She said she had a lot of trauma."

"Do you know if she was abused?"

"Let me just say, I believe she was."

"I assumed everyone knew she was hitting me."

"No. She never shared. That would have ended our friendship. Honestly, though, I felt things were not right. I did ask why she seemed to not be so good to you. Even at the time her response was unacceptable. But I let it go. Forgive me."

"Thank you. I don't blame you or anyone else."

"I regret not pushing the issue. I would have done something, had I known the extent of what was going on."

Later, after thinking, she responded in more detail. "Linda was abused both mentally and physically by her parents. She never felt she was good enough. In fact, she had many issues. I tried to be there for her. But she had her own way of doing things, and if you didn't agree with her, it didn't go well."

This interaction was very helpful to me. I'm still processing it, actually.

I guess the takeaway is this: Abuse is contagious. Do your best not to expose your children to it if you don't want them to pass it on to others one day.

––––––––

Did I ever stop drinking? No. I told you it probably wasn't that sort of book.

However, when I drink now, it's one or two. Ever since that night in DC when I tripped on psilocybin and saw a tentacled monster made of fabric eat my memory of Linda, the compulsion to binge is gone. I like to drink with friends. I like a Manhattan at a nice bar at the end of a crazy day.

I believe in harm reduction as opposed to abstinence. I don't keep hard liquor in the house. I keep a case of Miller Lite in the fridge for the days I'm feeling especially anxious. As far as I'm concerned, that's basically bottled water. But I never drink more than two.

I've stopped smoking pot every night. Eventually I realized it was mostly the weed that was causing the weight gain. It was the damned munchies. Fourth meal was invented by potheads. As soon as I cut back, I was less hungry.

I replaced the pot with nicotine. After I returned from Pipestone, Minnesota, I started smoking my catlinite pipe in my office. Eventually I replaced it with a meerschaum pipe. There's this tobacco shop down the road that hand-mixes its own blends that smell like cherry and whiskey. That, of course, became intolerable to the rest of the family and so I switched to a vape. I figure my lungs can take over the heavy lifting my liver has been doing for a while.

If you've found a way to navigate this world without chemical assistance, I applaud you.

I have had no suicidal ideations for many months. Those loops of negative thoughts have vanished, too. I believe the psychedelics did most of that. Mindfulness and meditation have helped tremendously as well.

Julie said something recently that helped me gain some perspective. "Your parents taught you how to never miss them," she said. My mother learned to not contact me during the weeks she didn't have custody of me, because the reminder of what we both lost hurt too much. And my father was busy working second shift at the factory and, later, running his construction firm. "But your kids would be devastated to lose you," she said. "You never left."

Until that moment I'd never considered that my not being here could hurt them. Strange, the things our minds never consider until someone explains the world to us.

right now

Last week Casey drove my car into the farmland south of Akron, to a summer camp managed by the YMCA. He got his temps in January and he drives me everywhere now. He takes it very seriously and reads driving manuals in his spare time. We practice maneuverability in the church parking lot by our house. It's beginning to dawn on me that he won't live with me forever, and that I will have to let him go, too. It scares me and thrills me at the same time. I can't wait to see what he makes of his life, what he makes of this strange world.

He wants to be a camp counselor. He signed up to be a CIT at camp this summer. I agreed to it because this YMCA camp is mostly run by women. And there are no secret societies that take kids into the woods to warn them about homosexuality.

Sometimes I think of all the trouble that could find him and I can barely breathe.

We pull into the gravel lot and I help him with his duffel bag, and the smells and the sounds take me back to Seven Ranges and all the dear friends I made and all the dangers we faced.

This summer will change him. And I'm here for it.

"Be careful," I say.

"I promise," he replies.

Photo by Alex Capaldi

This summer will change him.

And I'm here for it.

acknowledgments

How do I thank the people I really want to thank? They are made-up names. Thanking pseudonyms seems like a pointless exercise. We were kids and now we're adults and we do important things and we have families and none of us want to be associated with the terrible things that happened at Seven Ranges in the summer of 1995.

Instead, I think I'll thank my parents.

I only saw my mother on alternating weekends when I was a kid, but I know she's the reason I'm a professional writer. On our weekends when she lived in Bedford with Tom, she would take me to the library on Saturday afternoons. I could get three books to take with me and the lending cycle was two weeks, so I could return them on our next visit. I learned to understand the Dewey decimal system enough to know that the books about unsolved mysteries were to be found right near the beginning. That's where I'd go every time. One of my favorite series of books was the Time-Life Mysteries of the Unknown collection. They were tall books with thick black covers with titles like, *Alien Encounters* and *Time and Space*. I would read them in bed at night on the farm and scare myself silly. The supposedly true stories I found in those books are the seeds of everything I've written.

My mother took me to symphonies and movies and plays and museums. And I brought some of that culture back to the country with me in between.

She started taking classes at the community college when I was twelve and chipped away at a bachelor's degree over the course of twenty years. She now has her master's, which is more than I ever earned. She did this after having four children and surviving so much abuse and trauma. Her journey, seen from the sidelines, was inspiring.

Thank you, Mom.

My father worked in the steel mills in Cleveland and then ran a construction company. After it went bankrupt, he went to work for his brother and built some more houses with him. In 2010, he ran for Congress as a Tea Party Democrat candidate for Ohio's Sixth District's primary. He and I canvassed the poor communities along the state's eastern border down to Marietta and got enough signatures to get him on the ballot. We made signs with cardboard and spray paint in his driveway. He earned 31 percent of the vote, spending absolutely no money on his campaign.

When I was young, my father showed me how to manage my anxiety, and I'm not sure what would have happened if he hadn't. I certainly wouldn't have taken the risks in life that later rewarded me with a career. "What's the worst that can happen?" he would say when I was dealing with some interpersonal drama in school. "They can't eat you." That's become one of my personal mantras to this day and it really does help put things in perspective sometimes.

I was probably twelve years old when he taught me how to conquer fear. I believe I told you about the Native American mounds in the woods behind our house. I had read one of those Time-Life books and I'd gotten it into my head that there were monsters out there among the mounds. I refused to go out to play anymore. I told my dad I was afraid that as soon as I was out of sight of the house, something would grab me and drag me down to hell, or worse. He took away my books until I walked out to the mounds by myself, to prove that there was nothing there. At first, I was sad, and then I was angry. I'll show him, I thought. I'll walk out there and get abducted by a zombie—and then won't he feel terrible! And so I walked into the woods, along a trail the deer used. I could feel my heart in my chest protesting. I don't know if you've ever been truly terrified in your life, but it's different than simple fear. Terror is cold. It takes over your mind and your body until you think you might just die from the shock of it. I climbed up onto the rock mound and stood still, waiting for the hands to come out from below and pull me in. But, of course, they never did. Only, that ruined my plan. How would I be able to make him feel bad, now that I was still alive? And so I went deeper into the forest. Surely, there were monsters back there. Demons. Vampires. Eldritch horrors. I walked all the way to the metal post that marked our property line and nothing happened. Eventually I went back home. My dad met me at the door.

"You didn't have to go so far," he said.

I didn't say anything. I couldn't let him know he'd won. I took my books back and went to my room. I was never afraid of the woods again.

It's been thirty-five years and I still think about that lesson, probably once a week.

Thank you, Dad.

discussion questions

1. The Boy Scouts of America was founded in 1910. William Howard Taft was president. A loaf of bread cost six cents. Women did not yet have the right to vote. Is there a place for such an old institution in modern day? Can the Boy Scouts of America survive for another one hundred years? Should they?

2. Many summer camps have honors programs and secret societ ies as part of their legacy. Some look at this as an important rite of passage that turns boys into men. Similar clubs, like the Elks and Moose fraternities, offer quiet community for like-minded grown men; many professionals, to this day, take part in the ancient society of the Freemasons. Is there a use for such secret groups? Was Pipestone really that bad?

3. Eighty-two thousand former Boy Scouts have filed for com- pensation from the Boy Scouts of America's settlement trust, each claiming different levels of abuse. The organization has implemented several changes to make abuse less likely, such as two-deep leadership and allowing women to lead troops. Given that participation in the Boy Scouts includes overnight camps in isolated locations, is there a level of supervision that could ever adequately limit the risk of potential abuse?

4. Since 1995, when much of this story takes place, the stigma against having mental health issues has changed radically. This book speaks frankly about issues such as depression and substance abuse. Is this openness helpful or is it too

triggering for potential readers? Would you recommend this book to a friend who was struggling with similar issues?

5. The central mystery of this book is the death of Mike Klingler and the question: What really happened to him? Renner concludes at the end that Klingler likely committed suicide, even though the medical examiner leaves open the possibility of murder. Given the evidence presented, what do you think happened to Mike Klingler?

6. The settlement fund set aside by the Boy Scouts of America is $2.6 billion. This will be distributed to victims of abuse within Scouting, based on severity of the abuse. As we learned in this book, one of the reasons the Boy Scouts are being forced to pay such a large sum is because unlike other youth organizations, they kept meticulous records of suspected abusers. Do you think this settlement arrangement was fair? Is there a better way to offer help to those who've suffered?

7. When Renner was eleven years old, he didn't question the strangeness of the Pipestone ceremonies. When you're that young, you tend to believe that if adults are doing it, it must be normal. Only with age and experience has the author come to realize how bizarre the whole thing was. Was there something in your childhood that you were a part of that you later came to realize was not normal at all?

8. Since the very beginning of the Boy Scouts, Native American traditions have been rewritten and misrepresented in some of their programs and ceremonies, especially in secret societies such as Pipestone and Mic-O-Say. Male leaders sometimes don feathered headdresses, paint their skin red, and wear loincloths. Should any part of Native American history be a part of Scouting today? Is there a responsible way to honor the history of indigenous people?

9. Eighty-two thousand Scouts have sued the BSA for the abuse they suffered as children. But the settlement funds only address monetary compensation. Childhood trauma manifests in many ways, through depression and anxiety, or other mental diseases. How should we be addressing this part of the problem? Do you think MDMA and psilocybin therapy should be made available to these victims, as well as military veterans suffering from PTSD? Why or why not?

10. Who is the true villain of this story?

further investigation

If you care to fall farther down the rabbit hole to learn more about the dark subjects of this book, here is a list of resources you might find helpful.

On the life of Lord Robert Baden-Powell and the creation of the Boy Scouts:

- Tim Jeal's *Baden-Powell* is an exhaustive exploration of the life of the man who invented Scouting, as we know it. He had access to Baden-Powell's personal letters, which the family has since withdrawn from public consumption.
- Mary Drewery's *Baden-Powell: The Man Who Lived Twice* is a slender volume and a solid, quick overview of the leader.

On Boy Scout tradition:

- *The Official Boy Scout Handbook* is one of the most successful books of all time, with 40 million copies in print. I prefer the Ninth Edition, which is the one I read, cover to cover, as a teen boy. If nothing else, you'll pick up some handy survival skills, like how to properly build a fire and how to gather rainwater for drinking.

On the abuse scandal within the Boy Scouts of America:

- *Scout's Honor: Sexual Abuse in America's Most Trusted Institution*, a book by journalist Patrick Boyle, explains how the abuse scandal within the Boy Scouts of America came to light (much of it was due to Boyle's early reporting).

- If you'd rather watch a documentary, I'd recommend starting with Hulu's *Leave No Trace: A Hidden History of the Boy
  Scouts.*

On the responsible use of psychedelics to treat mental disorders:
- Nobody knows this growing field quite like Dr. Rick Doblin,
  founder of the Multidisciplinary Association for Psychedelic
  Studies. Check out his book, *Manifesting Minds: A Review of
  Psychedelics in Science, Medicine, Sex, and Spirituality.*

On Mindfulness and Meditation:
- I found two books to be very helpful in my quest to deal
  with the existential dread of reality: *Happiness: A Guide to
  Developing Life's Most Important Skill,* by molecular-biolo-
  gist-turned-Buddhist-monk Matthieu Ricard, and *The Subtle
  Art of Not Giving a F*ck,* by Mark Manson. Whatever trauma
  you may have experienced, these books teach you how to
  live easier.

resources

For survivors of abuse within the Boy Scouts of America, you are
not alone. There are over eighty-two thousand men ready to stand
behind you. If you want to learn more about how to file a claim,
or if you need resources to help manage your trauma, please visit
SurvivingScouting.org for more information.